"God is calling Christian wom[...]ful, and fruitful—in a hundred significant good w[...] p[...] the universe existed. Abigail Dodds is a proven voice for truth among today's cacophony of counsel for women. Her passion is that women love being God-centered, Christ-exalting, Bible-saturated women. This is not the portrait of womanhood painted by the world. Therefore, she is calling not for something easy, but for something courageous. I hope you consider her challenge."

John Piper, Founder and Teacher, desiringGod.org; Chancellor, Bethlehem College & Seminary; author, *Desiring God*

"*(A)Typical Woman* reminds readers to break the mold of Christian stereotypes while resisting the untrue, pliable ideas of the world. This is a deep, thought-provoking read that challenges us to find our identity in Christ alone."

Emily Jensen and **Laura Wifler,** Cofounders, Risen Motherhood

"Abigail Dodds presents a gospel-centered and gospel-saturated approach to the topic of womanhood. She points women to our identity in Christ and encourages, challenges, and exhorts us to live in light of our union with Christ. This book is for any woman in any season."

Kristin Schmucker, Founder and CEO, The Daily Grace Co.; Bible study author

"Every Christian woman will benefit from reading *(A)Typical Woman*. In it, Abigail Dodds gently corrects false beliefs about womanhood, encouraging us to embrace God's true design for Christian women by centering our entire person around Christ. Dodds's words refreshed and encouraged me not only to embrace but to actually enjoy my design as a woman of God."

Hunter Beless, Host, *Journeywomen* podcast

"Our generation suffers from amnesia. We don't remember who we are or why we were created, and that is why, sadly, we have settled for a distorted reality. This book is an elixir against the terrible disease that causes us to forget who we are as women and what our womanhood is really about. I invite you to read it to discover the truth or to remember it. This book is a timely reminder of truth to women living in a forgetful generation. In *(A)Typical Woman*, Abigail Dodds's words are filled with truth, grace, and great insight."

Betsy Gómez, Blogger, Revive Our Hearts Hispanic Outreach

(A)Typical Woman

(A)Typical Woman

Free, Whole, and Called in Christ

Abigail Dodds

WHEATON, ILLINOIS

Scripture quotations are from the ESV® Bible (The Holy Bible, English Standard Version®), copyright © 2001 by Crossway, a publishing ministry of Good News Publishers. Used by permission. All rights reserved.

Trade paperback ISBN: 978-1-4335-6269-3
ePub ISBN: 978-1-4335- 978-1-4335-6272-3
PDF ISBN: 978-1-4335-6270-9
Mobipocket ISBN: 978-1-4335-6271-6

Library of Congress Cataloging-in-Publication Data

Names: Dodds, Abigail, 1981- author.
Title: (A)Typical woman : free, whole, and called in Christ / Abigail Dodds.
Other titles: Typical woman
Description: Wheaton, Illinois : Crossway, [2019] | Includes bibliographical references and index.
Identifiers: LCCN 2018023820 (print) | LCCN 2018039649 (ebook) | ISBN 9781433562709
    (pdf) | ISBN 9781433562716 (mobi) | ISBN 9781433562723 (epub) | ISBN 9781433562693 |
    ISBN 9781433562693 (trade paperback : alk. paper) | ISBN 9781433562723 (ePub) | ISBN
    9781433562709 (PDF) | ISBN 9781433562716 (Mobipocket)
Subjects: LCSH: Women—Religious aspects—Christianity. | Christian women—Religious life.
Classification: LCC BT704 (ebook) | LCC BT704 .D58 2019 (print) | DDC 248.8/43—dc23
LC record available at https://lccn.loc.gov/2018023820

Crossway is a publishing ministry of Good News Publishers.

LB		29	28	27	26	25	24	23	22	21	20	19
15	14	13	12	11	10	9	8	7	6	5	4	3	2	1

For you have died,
and your life is hidden with Christ in God.
When Christ who is your life appears,
then you also will appear with him in glory.
Colossians 3:3–4

For my children, my joy, may Christ be your life.
And for Tom, our anchor and our wind.

Contents

Introduction

See that you fulfill the ministry that you have received
in the Lord. *Colossians 4:17*

My name is Abigail, a name my dad gave me. I'm the youngest of
four kids, born and raised in southeastern Iowa. My parents brought
us up in a small North American Baptist church where I heard the
gospel (repeatedly over the years), repented, and believed around
the age of twelve or so. I was baptized and discipled. I never knew
that there was such a thing as life apart from serving God. What I
mean by that is that while my parents have never been employed
by a church, they've also never not served the Lord in whatever they
do, inside the church and outside.

I tell you this so that you can understand why I would endeavor
to write a book on Christian womanhood. After all, any woman who
sets out to write about being a Christian woman must have everything figured out (ha) or be a glutton for punishment. I do recall
when I first had an inkling to write a book and the thought flashed
through my mind, "As long as it isn't on womanhood! That's something I never want to write on!" Has ever a topic been so fixated on,
maligned, idolized, marginalized, criticized, and generally made
a mess of? Well, yes, other topics are as fraught. But still, it ranks.

And what right do I have to wade into such waters? I have no right. I, like my parents before me and my children after me, have simply been given gifts. They aren't gifts I chose, and they aren't gifts I earned. First, I was given the gift of belonging to God through Jesus and then the gift of ministry that he gives to all believers in his varied forms. One form it has taken in my life is writing and teaching other women. This book is part of my service, my calling, my joy, and the outworking of my life in Christ.

This is a simple book written by a simple woman who is writing with skin in the game during the middle of the second quarter. The chapters you are about to read were written in real time as I faced real questions about what it means to be a Christian woman, with occasional angst and tense moments and frustrations, with my head in God's Book while my hands served my family and tried to live out things I didn't fully understand. It was drafted with near constant interruptions and the recurring deletion of social media apps from my phone. It was typed with dough under my fingernails and revised amidst conflict, repentance, and forgiveness. It's a book not of abstract ideas but of sweaty eye-balled real life.

But it was also written with deepening thankfulness and overwhelming peace and awestruck worship at what God has done in making us women and claiming us for his own. It was written amid the laughter that comes from knowing God really is in control—whether I fully understand his ways or not. I did not write a manifesto but, rather, meditations on a theme. My aim is to understand Christian womanhood as both God's word and God's world have revealed it to us—that is, to understand it as created through Jesus and for him. So each chapter stands alone as it narrows in on one aspect of things, and all the chapters come together to help give shape to our understanding of Christian women who are women through and through (part 1) and in all they do (part 2), and who are fearless and free in Christ (part 3).

I have not mastered the content of this book. No, but I am in the process of being mastered by it, insomuch as it expresses the reality and truth that must eventually master us all. I wrote the book I need—which is why it may occasionally make your toes curl. I've found that grace isn't something I can't give to myself by going easy on myself or by asking others to go easy on me. I'm not the one I should be going to for grace at all. But administering the grace of God found *in Christ* is a vast deal better than going easy on myself. With Christ, toe-curling hard truths become life-giving tonics.

Parts of this book were inspired both positively and negatively by past and current teaching in Christian circles on the topic—some that glorified womanhood for its own sake, some that belittled it, and much of which compartmentalized it. I found the compartmentalizing of womanhood (where being a woman is understood merely as certain feminine ideals) to be the catalyst for both its inappropriate glorification (*Let's make femininity our entire life!*) and its belittling (*Let's rise above womanhood as important humans, not silly women!*). But when we can understand being a woman as a full reality that is in our fingers and toes as much as in our wombs and breasts, we begin to see that we must read our womanhood, both in the text of Scripture and the text of our lives, through the cross—through Christ himself. I want women to be at peace as women, to be grateful for being made women, and to see it all as an essential part of Christ's mission and work.

I also hope that this book will be a tool in discipleship and growth in the Lord for young women and old women and whoever picks it up. Even as I seek to be a help, I can't replace your flesh-and-blood brothers and sisters in Christ. It is in that context—the context of relationship, accountability, authority, and community—that tools like this book find a happy, useful home.

Yet author to reader and reader to author, we are entering into a sort of relationship with trust. It's a limited trust, to be sure, precisely because many of you don't know me and I don't know you, and because all human trust is limited. We have only one fully trustworthy person in our lives: our triune God. Yet human trust is necessary and ought to be present in our relationships as we imitate our Savior and seek to walk in the light together. So as I enter this trust with you, reader, I want to be upfront about what I'm asking from you. I'm asking for more than passive engagement. I ask for biblical discernment alongside a willingness to put your pet horses in the stall for the next seventeen chapters. I confess to you that I've got plenty of pet ponies and preferences that I've tried to make the template for godliness, but it just won't do. It leads only to a reshaping of God in my image, something that is more frightening than anything God asks of me.

So many are searching for a novel approach, a new way to think about something, a uniqueness or niche. But if you live long enough, you realize that novelty isn't a virtue. Novelty causes cancer: mutating cells doing what they shouldn't. Novelty causes gene abnormalities and disability—a reality with which I'm quite familiar. In the world of ideas, it's often just dressed-up ignorance of all the bad ideas that have already been tried. Novelty leads to heresy and false teaching. Novelty leads to trying to look cool and be unique, which happens to be exactly what everyone else is doing and has always done. I'm looking for something fixed and dependable. I find it in God and his Word, the only way you can be made new by an unchanging God and his ancient Book.

I don't intend for this book to be a novelty. But I have noticed that in our distraction and obsession with what's trending, often the ancient truth is forgotten. When we resurrect it, it seems new to us. If this book seems like new information to you, it isn't because I came up with something novel; it's because we've forgotten the basics, or we were never taught them. When we receive the reality of God and the gospel, the realities of life in Christ as a woman start to take shape. That's what I want to explore with you. I'm hoping that we would, with poet George Herbert, learn to live here on earth with one eye to heaven and with the realization that our lives are hid there in Christ (Col. 3:3). Look to find yourself there.

MY words and thoughts do both express this notion,
That LIFE hath with the sun a double motion.
The first IS straight, and our diurnal friend:
The other HID, and doth obliquely bend.
One life is wrapt IN flesh, and tends to earth;
The other winds t'wards HIM whose happy birth
Taught me to live here so THAT still one eye
Should aim and shoot at that which IS on high—
Quitting with daily labour all MY pleasure,
To gain at harvest an eternal TREASURE.[1]

PART 1

WOMEN THROUGH AND THROUGH—IN CHRIST

In the beginning was the Word, and the Word was with God, and the Word was God. He was in the beginning with God. All things were made through him, and without him was not any thing made that was made. *John 1:1–3*

1

The Meaning of Words: *Christian* and *Woman*

Therefore, if anyone is in Christ, he is a new creation.
The old has passed away; behold, the new has come.
2 Corinthians 5:17

So God created man in his own image,
   in the image of God he created him;
      male and female he created them. *Genesis 1:27*

Language has this tendency to morph and change over time. It's not necessarily a bad thing; new words are created and others become outdated, so a woman saying "I pray thee" in the eighteenth century now would simply say "please." The meaning isn't lost in the change. But not all language can or should morph. There are some words that God has given us to hold onto. They're his words for things. *Christian* and *woman* are two of those words. No doubt both of them have fallen on hard times.

Someone could choose to write about a number of other words that God has given us, so why pick those two? I suppose because of how relevant they are for me and how far I've had to come in my understanding of them, even as I live them—and how far I still have to go. When God names something, he imbues it with his created and assigned meaning, and it's a fearful thing to go around changing the name or the meaning of something authored by God. It just so happens that he's called me "Christian" and "woman." And if you're reading this, it's likely what he has called you too.

I increasingly encounter Christian women who are unacquainted with the breadth and depth of the terms and how they relate, settling for caricatures, shadows, and distortions. And as I grow in my understanding of the two terms, I find that while it is possible to be a woman and not a Christian, it is not possible, for me, to be a Christian as anything other than a woman. That may be ridiculously obvious, but we live in an age where the obvious is obscure.

Even those who call themselves "Christian" can be confusing in their messages about these words' meanings, from articles to books to women's talks to sermons. Some agree with each other; some strongly disagree. How do we sort out these competing messages among Christians? How do we hold on to what's true and let the chaff blow away? I know of only one way: the wisdom given by God's Holy Spirit through the potent dosing of God's Word in the midst of God's people. If our convictions and our very lives are not breathed out by God's Spirit, rooted in his Word, we will be confused by the mass of articulate, funny, and appealing messages that come at us. We will likely gravitate toward the ones that most resonate with our personal preferences. Or our sin bent.

Bravery with the World or the Word?

I'm partly distressed over the state of Christian women. I see women who have abandoned their reason, their moral agency, and their God-fearing courage to follow people who tell them just what they want to hear (messages that are strikingly similar to the trends of our time), attending online churchy clubs and plastering half-true platitudes all over social media. I see women's conferences filled with relatable personalities, side-splitting monologues, and new false doctrines that are actually as old as the garden of Eden and Eve herself.

They revere a self-styled bravery that is anything but brave, "courageously" calling sin beautiful in agreement with the world, rather than standing firm in the minority of Bible-believing people who must set themselves stable and steadfast in each era's cultural tornado. Empathy is their idol; feelings the new Baal. They imagine that the sorrow and distancing of fellow Christians from them is proof of their solidarity with Jesus, when really it's the fruit of a desperate and impossible friendship with the world that God's children are forbidden to take part in. And we can't be surprised by it. Not only because all of us are sinful, but because in some places the church has become a bastion of the perfect rather than the gathering of the needy. This has sounded a dissonant note in the hearts of many women, causing them to search out new interpretations on truth. Let's beckon them home. Not to the hollow, culturally Christian tombs called "church"—polished on the outside but dead where it counts—but to the incomparable, uncompromising Jesus, the true Shepherd of the sheep.

I'm also encouraged. I'm encouraged by the women who show up to study God's Word week in and week out, young women who are sick to death of the fluff, who know that a half-truth is more dangerous than a full-out lie and refuse to remain infants in their thinking. I'm encouraged by women who, rather than follow their feelings, lead those feelings around by the sound of God's voice in the Bible. This book is for them. And it's for the rest of us who need a refresher course that blows gospel air into our stale hearts, reminding us what life in Christ as a woman looks like.

To some, *Christian* means nothing more than being born south of the Mason-Dixon Line to folks who used to go to church, and there's a plaque on a pew somewhere to prove it. Where I'm from in Minnesota, being a Christian means being nice and indirect, never disagreeing with people except in the cloak of passive-aggressiveness. Many of us opt for adjectives to help give clarity to the word *Christian*, such as *serious*, *Bible-believing*, *born-again*, *evangelical*, *Reformed*, and so on. Some toss it in the dust bin and try to think up a cool-sounding synonym.

Erasing Women

The word *woman* is equally distressing, if not more. In our society, being a woman is increasingly based on our sense of ourselves rather than on what God has assigned us to be, so it's hard to know what is meant by the term. Among some feminists, a woman is someone with few, if any, meaningful differences from man—except that she likely views women as a victim of "gendered society."[2] Her biology is of little to no significance; her mind is everything—as if our female minds can overcome gender, which even secular science reminds us is not the case.[3] This echo of Gnosticism makes bodies irrelevant and embraces a mind-over-matter dictum.[4]

What we have left is a woman whose intellect is detached from her body, who tries to ignore biological and physical reality. This can account for women vying for a spot on men's sports teams, with an absolutized belief that they can be whatever they put their mind to. It also accounts for those, perhaps few, eager for a place in military combat. And it even accounts for bright women who try to detach from their bodies to use them for sex, money, and power.

The transgender thinking goes farther, not ignoring reality but actively redefining it. For some people who consider themselves transgender, most famously showcased by Bruce Jenner's change to Caitlyn, becoming a woman may mean wearing feminine clothes, having plastic surgeries to construct womanly anatomy, taking hormones and drugs to suppress other hormones, and speaking in a womanly voice, with a hyper-feminine affect. In other words, and with no sense of irony, being a woman is often the opposite of what it means to modern feminists.

It is alarming to some older feminists that their labor to bring forth a better world for women ended up giving birth to a movement that seeks the annihilation of women altogether. The younger generation doesn't seem to mind, however, and are quickly working to bridge the gap between feminism and transgenderism, so that Bruce Jenner's expression of transgenderism (a man becoming super feminine in mostly superficial ways) is less in vogue than the logical next step of genderlessness, or genderqueer identity.[5] One detail that we should observe is that the movement toward gender fluidity in all its forms harms women and children. It harms men too. But it is insidious in how it removes protection and creates added vulnerability for women and children. The attempt to abolish or blur the sexes will fail, as nature—that is, our Father's world—has a way of being intractable. But in the trying, many women are being and will be damaged by themselves or others.

Recycled Sin, Repeated History, Unchanging Christ

These cultural winds should not shock us, nor should they produce in us knee-jerk reactions as though sin, especially sexual sin, were a new or foreign idea. It's been around from the beginning. My own sinfulness, my own proclivities toward evil, ensure my compassion for those who have not received Christ as Lord and are walking in darkness (Eph. 2:1–3). And the pain and confusion men and women experience as they spend their lives feeling shackled by their sex, or defined by sexual orientation or an unwanted fixation on an internal sense of gender, should secure our action to bring the gospel to them. The pain and confusion we all experience before coming to Christ is inextricably linked with our hatred and rejection of God, which is also a type of hatred of ourselves. We hate what God has done—he has made us a particular way, and we want to be self-makers (Rom. 1:24–25). The gospel is the only hope of peace for all of us.

Within Christianity, we also see some moving toward defining femaleness as a role that we inhabit rather than as an ontological, whole-person category.[6] It is as though we relegate our sex to our uterus and uniquely female parts, the same way we relegate our womanhood to the passages of Scripture that directly address women rather than understanding that the XX chromosomes span head, shoulders, knees, and toes—and that we are always addressed as women, whether directly or indirectly, in a broad sense, by all of Scripture.

Thankfully God's spoken Word, the Bible, and his spoken word in creation give substance to these words—*Christian* and *woman*—with all the precision and clarity that the world, which has closed its eyes to "the things that have been made" (Rom. 1:20), needs. And both have done so through the ages, undeterred as new waves of so-called enlightenment crash against their unchanging shoreline.

If the roots of our ideals for Christian women can be traced to an imaginary 1950s suburban utopia or the pride of the antebellum era or Jane Austen's clever Lizzy Bennett or reactionary feminism or career-driven urban centers or any place other than in the one man, Jesus Christ, the fruit on our tree will be rotten. There is only one seed out of which Christian women grow, and that seed isn't an American ideal; it is the imperishable seed of Christ, and it is able to grow in every place and people in the world.

Our Christianity and our womanhood are two things that aren't going away. Don't you think it's worth our time to try to understand them the way God does?

Discussion Questions

1. What is your understanding of the word *Christian*? Who and what define it for you?

2. What is your understanding of the word *woman*? Who and what define it for you?

3. How does the culture around you define these words? Do those definitions match with God's definitions?

2

The End Is the Beginning

And he is before all things, and in him all things hold together. *Colossians 1:17*

. . . even as he chose us in him before the foundation of the world. *Ephesians 1:4*

When most of us come to Christ, we know relatively little about him. Likely we haven't even read all of his Book. But what we do know is indescribably good news, and it is enough to secure our eternal devotion.

What we know when we come to Christ is the end of the story, as far as the Bible is concerned. We know the gospel, which came into full view in the last third of Scripture. Even those of us raised on Scripture, when we come to Christ, our coming is still located at the end of the Book. And as we find ourselves new, reborn, and in Christ, having begun at the end, we go back and learn or relearn all about God's story—his creation, his plan, his promises—which has now become our story. We read how Christ was there from the beginning and that God made everything through Christ (John 1:1–3), how we were chosen in Christ before the foundation of the world (Eph. 1:4), how Christ was everywhere (Luke 24:27)—popping up visibly and invisibly—and how that's now *our* family history. It's like children asking to hear the story of how they were born and how their parents and grandparents met. They need someone else to recount it or show them the photo albums or baby books. And they never, ever get tired of hearing it.

So rather than understand ourselves as first women and all that entails and then Christians, it actually works the opposite way. Without Christ, we can know what we ought to be as women because of the clear signs given to us in creation and in our created bodies, but we will be powerless to be what we ought. Even more than that, we will be at war with God and his creation. We must first be found in Christ in order to humbly and happily receive both the revelation of God's world and his Word. We can never come to the Old Testament, even the creation account, and expect to understand it rightly without the revelation of Jesus Christ. That's who the whole book is about, after all. So that's where we begin.

The gospel of Jesus Christ is something a young child can understand, but its complexity and ramifications are inexhaustible. It is that God, who created everything and everyone (Gen. 1:1), sent his Son (1 John 4:14), who is also God (John 8:58), to earth to be born as a man named Jesus (Matt. 1:21). He did this out of his great love for us (Eph. 2:4), because our sin made us his enemies; his Son Jesus came to make peace for us (Rom. 5:1, 10). The way Jesus made this peace was by living a holy, perfect, and sinless life (2 Cor. 5:21), then being crucified by wicked people like us and dying a terrible death on a cross (Luke 23). When he died, he took the punishment for all the sins of those who put their trust in him—past, present, and future (Rom. 3:21–26). He was buried in a tomb, and three days later, God raised him from the dead, and he appeared to many in his resurrected body (Acts 2:32; 1 Cor. 15:6). Then God took him up to heaven, where Christ is now seated at the right hand of God the Father (Luke 24:51; Col. 3:1).

All who repent of their sin, die to themselves, and believe in him are given eternal life and the righteousness of Christ (Luke 24:47; Rom. 6:5–14). They are also given God's Holy Spirit, who was sent as a helper for us, to guide us in the truth (John 14:16–17). And even in this life, our lives are now lived in the death-conquering Christ, as though eternity has already begun (Col. 3:3–4). We are transformed, brand new, and born-again (2 Cor. 3:18; 2 Cor. 5:17; 1 Pet. 1:3).

This is the gospel. It is the end of the story—which is just where all good stories really begin.

An Onion or an Apple Tree

There's a real risk for us though, even as we embrace the gospel, that we will make it a story that's mainly about us. *Our* self-discovery, *our* journey, *our* triumph. We Christians have this knack for cramming the gospel into one short act of a play that merely enhances the bigger epic tale starring yours truly. We all crave self-knowledge: "Who am I?" or for some, "What's unique about me?" And we tend to make those the central plot points of our lives.

The process of discovery often looks like an attempt to climb inside our belly buttons and peer through any cracks to the innards. Maybe then we'll know who we are and why we're special. We think of ourselves like an onion with oh-so-many layers, and as we peel them back, we are as beguiled as Mr. Tumnus in C. S. Lewis's *The Last Battle*: "'Yes,' said Mr. Tumnus, 'like an onion: except that as you continue to go in and in, each circle is larger than the last.'"[7] But rather than being in the real Narnia beholding better glory after better glory, we're utterly captivated by the navel-lint idol of self. Even those of us who don't like ourselves are often still captive to the fixation of *self*.

The inundation of online personality tests is enough to keep us busily navel gazing for days on end. We can unearth what Disney princess best matches our disposition, whether we are an introvert or an extrovert and the vast ways we've been misunderstood as a result of that. We can discover our strengths and learn that our Myers-Briggs type has us in the rare 1 percent of personalities! And even more, we can share our newfound knowledge of self with all our Facebook friends, so they too can revel in us. I suppose we could call it navel-gazing's underbelly. But real self-knowledge comes from knowing God, from looking out, not in.

So how do we rightfully acknowledge the actual categories of our lives that exist and make us uniquely us without engaging in a narcissistic fixation on *Ten Things Every Introvert Needs from Others to Be Happy?* We really are composed of something—the sum of the life we've lived, our roles and talents. In that scheme, our onion layers might include categories such as daughter, sister, friend, victim, mom, wife, single, divorced, musician, expert of such and such, communicator, and on and on, depending on the sum of *your* life experience, talents, and roles. And if you're a Christian, you may think of the most foundational layer or the core of the onion as "Christian," and that layer is the key component of who you are.

But consider a different picture.

Rather than imagine yourself an autonomous onion on the counter of life, composed of complex layers, consider an apple tree.

A seed has gone into the ground and died. And from that dead seed, life has sprung up. It has grown thick and tall, rooted and established. On that tree are branches, leaves, buds, and fruit. The seed that fell into the ground and died is Christ. And when we become a Christian, that seed is also you and me, hidden in Christ and connected to every part of him, all his people. There are no Christians alone on the counter; only Christians growing together, in Christ.

Reckoned Dead

The problem with our identity may be that it hasn't yet died. We still think of ourselves as ourselves. I can hear my own objections saying, "But if I'm not me, then what? Don't I matter? What about my uniqueness? What about the life I've lived that *only* I've lived?" And the answer I find in Scripture is that it all must be reckoned dead.

When we participate in Christ's death, we die, every bit. It isn't that the sinful part of us dies and the nonsinful part endures, so that on the other side we're still us but with a makeover. There is no nonsinful part. And on the other side, having been raised with Christ, we aren't still us. We are entirely new, entirely in Christ.

John Bunyan says it best in *The Pilgrim's Progress*: "My name is now Christian, but my name at the first was Graceless."[8]

So for a woman, this means she dies as a mother, a friend, a daughter, and a coworker. The musician, the expert, the single and the divorced, all the things from our past that comprise us, our talents and person are all reckoned dead, as they were all tainted with sin, and are raised now as something else entirely. We are now Christian friend, Christian daughter, Christian wife, Christian divorced, Christian single. We are Christian women. We are not layers to be peeled back in order to get to the essence; every piece of us is new. We do not get to the core part of us where our Christian selves reside, but the core is the whole. All of life through, in, and for Christ (Col. 1:16).

Where, Not Who

But your life may not feel all brand new. The old self, the old sin, and all the past experiences may not feel transformed in Christ. Yes, sin lingers. And all of our lives are spent on this: becoming who we are in Christ. Being as tart and sweet and crisp and juicy as an apple should be. Being a woman whose nurture and love reflects

God's never-tiring nurture and love for us. Being a friend whose loyalty and faithfulness reflect Christ's loyalty to his Father and faithfulness to do his will. Being a mom whose promise keeping and steady instruction reflect the God who always keeps his promises and patiently instructs his children. Being a victim whose pain and heart reflect the way Christ's pain and heart was brought to his Father, tenderly cared for and listened to, even as the Father raised his Son from the dead.

Sometimes the question isn't *who* am I, but *where.* Where are you right now? Are you at home? At work? Eating supper? Reading in bed? At a coffee shop with Wi-Fi scrolling on your phone? At a park or the store? Know this: wherever you are, whatever you're doing, whatever jobs and talents and roles you have, you are in Christ, and all those things about you are in him. They belong to him. They're on his tree. They're for him; they're by him.

Let's crawl out of the despair that comes from trying to find ourselves. Die to that person, that smallness, that futility. "Look for yourself," warns Lewis, "and you will find in the long run only hatred, loneliness, despair, rage, ruin, and decay. But look for Christ and you will find Him, and with Him everything else thrown in."[9]

Discussion Questions

1. Do you consider yourself a Christian? Based on what?

2. Is your life oriented toward God—who he is, his Book, and his ways? Or, is it oriented on yourself and your identity?

3. How can you turn your focus to God and away from the fixation of self?

3

Wholly Women

He is the image of the invisible God, the firstborn of all creation. For by him all things were created, in heaven and on earth, visible and invisible, whether thrones or dominions or rulers or authorities—all things were created through him and for him. *Colossians 1:15–16*

Elisabeth Elliot said, "I don't want anybody treating me as a 'person' *rather* than as a woman. Our sexual differences are the terms of our life, and to obscure them in any way is to weaken the very fabric of life itself. Some women fondly imagine a new beginning of liberty, but it is in reality a new bondage, more bitter than anything they seek to be liberated from."[10]

Elisabeth has no trouble packing a punch. And I think she's right that if we have to choose between being treated as a person *or* as a woman, we should choose woman, because being a woman *is* the expression of our personhood. If I am treated as a woman, I *am* being treated as a person. But, if I'm thought of only as a human or a person, and being a woman is made irrelevant or small or distinct from that, something has run afoul.

We have some digging to do to fully understand what Elisabeth Elliot meant and why it matters, while we simultaneously and with enthusiasm agree with Dorothy Sayers that women are indeed human. The creation account is where we must turn.

> Then God said, "Let us make man in our image, after our likeness. And let them have dominion over the fish of the sea and over the birds of the heavens and over the livestock and over all the earth and over every creeping thing that creeps on the earth."
>
> > So God created man in his own image,
> > > in the image of God he created him;
> > > male and female he created them. (Gen. 1:26–27)

In the six-day creation account, we see God creating humanity. In accordance with his image we were made man and woman. Humanity is composed of male and female.

> The man gave names to all livestock and to the birds of the heavens and to every beast of the field. But for Adam there was not found a helper fit for him. So the LORD God caused a deep sleep to fall upon the man, and while he slept took one of his ribs and closed up its place with flesh. And the rib that the LORD God had taken from the man he made into a woman and brought her to the man. Then the man said,
>
> > "This at last is bone of my bones
> > > and flesh of my flesh;
> > she shall be called Woman,
> > > because she was taken out of Man." (Gen. 2:20–23)

One very obvious thing in these narratives that may be subtly overlooked in our good desire to live as more than a list of distinctly feminine ideals is that God doesn't create a human as anything but a man or a woman. I was not made a human mainly, with a side of woman. My humanity doesn't mean something bigger or more than having been made a woman; rather, I was made a woman as the expression of my humanity. I do not, cannot, exist except as a woman. And if you're a woman, neither do you.

What Part Is Human? What Part Is Woman?

If you are tempted to believe that being a woman is just one aspect of yourself, just one facet of who you are, and that a part of you is more than that, something above it or underneath it, something better than it, you are thinking too meanly of the word. You need a bigger category for God's creation called "woman."

Why is it a loss for me or you to be thought of as a human *rather* than as a woman? Isn't the point behind emphasizing our humanity to show that we have more than womanly stuff to offer? Something deeper, like our mind and personality? Aren't we created in God's image? Aren't we people too? And I want to answer, with the Bible, unequivocally yes! Yes! Women are people! Women are human! Women are image bearers! And I'm so thankful for the Christian women who've emphasized this and brought it to the fore in recent years, at a time when it seemed to almost have been forgotten in some corners.

It makes sense that we would want to minimize our womanhood to a part, rather than viewing it as something that encompasses the whole, if the only way we could embrace being an image bearer is to emphasize our humanity over the man-made idea of a little woman who is confined and defined only by a feminine role. In other words, what if we have a false understanding of all that a woman actually is? What if we are equating being a woman with our perception of femininity or with particular roles such as wife and mother?

We may have traded the fullness of God's creation of woman for our own small stereotype of her. The overlap between the stuff of a man and the stuff of a woman is remarkable and large and full and complex and a mystery. After all, we were taken from man; we are made of the same substance. When Adam first sees Eve in the garden, his delight in their similarity pours out poetically, "bone of my bones and flesh of my flesh" (Gen. 2:23).[11]

And so, because we see that there is a remarkable amount of sameness between a man and a woman, we may wrongly put the overlap of sameness in the category of "human" and then relegate the distinctive parts to the categories "man" and "woman," rather than seeing ourselves as wholly Christian and wholly woman. Plenty of our life will be spent *as a woman* in the shared responsibilities and shared roles between man and woman.

We share dominion; we are coheirs and disciples; we both have arms and hands and can unload the dishwasher with equal talent. But that doesn't make what *we* do less womanly or merely human. We unload the dishwasher as women. Does it change how the dishes get to the cupboards? No, and as some of you can probably attest, yes. We read the news as women. We go to meetings as women. We email and text and communicate as women. We may do all these things similarly to men, but somehow it still doesn't make us merely human. It simply lets us know that women are robust, capable people, just like men are. When my husband changes a diaper, he's still a man. Just because the task of diapering is often done by the mom, it doesn't make him a mom when he does it. Nor does he leave behind manhood when he does so and enter into a third transcendent realm of humanity. He changes the diaper as a man. Because he is and always will be a man—a human man.

What Makes a Real Woman?

Why does all this even matter? Who cares if we put ourselves in the category of human mainly and woman as a facet of that? Nobody's denying their womanhood; they're just trying to focus on the important stuff, not just the womanly stuff. I support some of that sentiment. But have you considered that everything we do is womanly, not because of the type of activity we're engaging in but precisely because we are women doing it?

The best reason I can give you for why we shouldn't think of being a woman as just a facet of ourselves is that God doesn't do it like that, and everything he does is for a good reason. *Being made a woman is not a morally neutral thing*; it goes down in the pro column. When he made us, he called us female and said, "Very good" (Gen. 1:31). He never indicates that it's something we ought to transcend through our humanity, because our womanhood *is* our humanity.

When we opt to see our womanhood as merely an aspect of ourselves, we make it small and unglorious, sometimes condemning it to a silly caricature. We actually degrade what God has made; we degrade ourselves. When we make the distinctive parts of womanhood the totality of it, we send a confusing message to our daughters and to the world. We tell them that being a woman is confined to those parts rather than showing them the breadth and depth of being wholly woman—even in the areas that overlap with men. So if they dislike dolls or never marry, they may start to wonder if their womanhood is defunct. With all the confusion in the world on this subject, the church has a message of hope, clarity, and love: *God made you a woman, and it is very good.* It is not confined to your position or career or to giving birth.

A wrong view of womanhood is further complicated by the Christian tendency to talk about being a *real* woman or a *real* man. From articles to books and more, Christians often admonish other Christians to be true or real men and women. This is their way of saying, "Be what God made you to be," or, "Be a *godly* man or woman"—which is really good and needed! But, unintentionally, calling people to be real men and women can send the message that if they don't behave a certain way, their femaleness or maleness is at stake—that God's creation of male and female is dependent on our ability to live it out rightly. It actually plays exactly to the transgender way of thinking. In the transgender mind-set, our internal sense of self dictates what we are. In the *real* men or women mindset, right behaviors or attitudes shape what we are. But it's not true. Our behaviors and attitudes indicate who we bow down to, but they can't dictate what we are. Only God can do that.

What makes real men and women is the fact that God made us men and women, just as what makes us real Christians is that God made us Christians by making us alive in Christ. In both cases, we don't earn it or achieve it or feel our way to it. *Being a Christian and being a woman are both gracious, given, God-spoken, unchangeable realities.*

Daughters in the Son

When we base our value on a category of transcendent humanity set against womanhood, we play into an anti-woman narrative that goes against God's very good design. But why not take the view God does? We matter because God made us *women in his image*, with all the complexities and overlap that entails. Fully women, fully valuable, fully his.

Growing up, I spent a vast amount of time with my closest friend, Lynette. She and I were often mistaken for each other because our mannerisms and ways became so similar after years of being together. We often would say the same things at the same times or think the same thoughts. But that didn't make me Lynette, and it didn't make her Abigail.

Likewise, we may think the same thoughts as men, with the same acuity, and we may do the same tasks with the same ability, but we do so as women, and they do so as men. To restrict the calling of either to the distinctions or differences (which are real and significant) lessens the calling of both. Men are called to train up their children; women are called to disciple the nations. Men are called to practice hospitality; women are called to work heartily as to the Lord, and vice versa. Much of our calling as men and women is interchangeable, but not all. The callings specific to women include being a helper, a wife, and a mom; teaching and training other women; prioritizing the home; and more (see Gen. 2:18; Titus 2:3–5). These callings are not the totality of our womanhood; they are *good* distinctives of it.

Let's not relegate womanhood to the edges of life and use the fact of our humanness to try to rise above it. Rather, let's reclaim and enjoy what we are and all that flows from it *in Christ:* holiness, meekness, a backbone of steel, fearlessness, love, giving life, strength, weakness, obedience, and much more. All of this comes from *what we are*: Christian women.

The world is in need of us. It needs women who understand the privilege and glory of being a woman. It needs women who are at peace in the body God has given them, at peace with paradoxical strengths and weaknesses, who don't demean what they were created as or, by extension, the Creator. What a story God is telling! And I, for one, am thankful to have the part of being wholly woman.

This understanding of ourselves as wholly women who are wholly in Christ makes these verses precious rather than a problem:

> In Christ Jesus you are all sons of God, through faith. For as many of you as were baptized into Christ have put on Christ. There is neither Jew nor Greek, there is neither slave nor free, there is no male and female, for you are all one in Christ Jesus. And if you are Christ's, then you are Abraham's offspring, heirs according to promise. (Gal. 3:26–29)

What a joy to know that being a daughter cannot hinder me from putting on the Son of God through faith! What a miracle to hear that my femaleness does not disqualify me from being an heir according to the promise given to the first Jewish man, Abraham. Rather than think that this is a call to throw off our being female and put on Christ, we can see that the beauty lies precisely in the diversity, not with flattening androgyny or muting of distinction.

Will there be Swedes in heaven? Will there be Africans? Latinos? Mongolians? Jews? Greeks? Yes. And aren't we thankful that God is more powerfully represented by uniting diversity to the praise of his glory? So it is with male and female. His revelation to us is that he is reflected by both. He gets more praise when women and men praise him. Man and woman are his image. But as women, we have the privilege of fully expressing our part. Without our full expression of it, we rob God of his full glory.

Manufactured Femininity

Both men and women have asked me what it looks like for women to actually live the way I just described—as wholly women—in the context of a predominantly male environment. In other words, when a woman steps into a meeting with all men, or even just mixed company in the classroom, at work, or at church, how does she somehow do that in a distinctly womanly way? How does she teach math as a woman? How does she make sure she's being womanly and not manly, acting in a way that befits her sex?

I know there aren't supposed to be any bad questions, but I think those are the wrong ones. If we were to answer them head on, it would lead to legalism and manufactured femininity, probably not Christlike women behaving like Christlike women. We'd start keeping a rule book of how often she can talk and whether she should be allowed to initiate discussions or contradict her male peers or professors. The location of the principles would be all wrong—on the outside instead of the inside. It could also lead to thinking of womanhood as something that *must* look different from manhood. But we can be women and act the same as men do in the classroom or at the office or the home. And when we do that, we aren't transcending our womanhood, nor are we being particularly masculine. We're being women. God made women just that robust.

A better question is: How can I live by faith as a *Christian* woman in every circumstance? The emphasis is on the word *Christian*. You cannot change that you are a woman, if that is what you are. Working out our new-creation-ness will grow us into godly women, not godly men, because that's what we are. Working out our salvation under the authority of God's Book will develop us into mature godly *women*. We need to trust God and trust the process of sanctification, not focus on manufacturing femininity. The way we do this is by being united to Christ in his life, death, and resurrection. It's by obeying these words:

> Put on then, as God's chosen ones, holy and beloved, compassionate hearts, kindness, humility, meekness, and patience, bearing with one another and, if one has a complaint against another, forgiving each other; as the Lord has forgiven you, so you also must forgive. And above all these put on love, which binds everything together in perfect harmony. (Col. 3:12–14)

When we do this, when we walk as Christians are exhorted to walk all through the New Testament, we won't need to fret about whether the distinctive parts of our womanhood are displayed well enough or displayed too much. We can trust that because we are in Christ, and we are following him and submitting to his Word, he will work in us what is good.

This doesn't mean we conveniently ignore the places in Scripture that direct our actions and behavior as women. Quite the contrary, we embrace them in the context they are given and apply them in all the ways they're meant to be applied.

We must remember that the more feminine virtues are not located first in women; they are located in God, because anything truly virtuous is found in him. So those places in the Bible that exhort women toward particular virtues may be considered more toward the feminine side of things, but that doesn't make them less a reflection of God. We are not trying to be something good that's different from the goodness and virtue we find in God. We are aiming to live what we are—Christians. We are women clothed in Christ's garments of holiness.

And that is not something we can manufacture with a rule book of feminine conduct. Trying to do such a thing will make for sickly, dim, judgmental women rather than robust, unflappable, and, yes, *beautiful*-on-the-inside Christian women who have firsthand knowledge of what God calls them to be: holy and wholly his.

Discussion Questions

1. Have you ever considered whether being a woman is just one part of you or encompasses all of you? What assumptions have you had about this?

2. Does being a woman seem like a confining or small reality to you? Why or why not?

3. How can you bring your thinking in line with what the Bible teaches about being made a woman?

4. Are you willing to submit yourself to God in how he made you, in both the fullness of being a woman and the limitedness of it?

4

Bible Women

Therefore, as you received Christ Jesus the Lord, so walk in him, rooted and built up in him and established in the faith, just as you were taught, abounding in thanksgiving. *Colossians 2:6–7*

Let the word of Christ dwell in you richly, teaching and admonishing one another in all wisdom, singing psalms and hymns and spiritual songs, with thankfulness in your hearts to God. *Colossians 3:16*

.

When I was seventeen years old, I read a book on the Proverbs 31 woman. I've no criticism to offer of the book. It was written by a godly woman who was pouring herself out in honoring God. I was electrified to discover a part of the Bible that seemed directly written for me, a female. It was the kind of discovery that felt like I was being given a template for life: no more mystery, no more puzzlement as I clumsily plowed through stuff I didn't understand—the step-by-step handbook had arrived.

When I combined what I'd read from Proverbs 31 with parts of the Bible that give instructions to women, I almost wasn't sure why

I needed to read the rest of the Bible. Maybe my job was to camp out here. Certainly there was enough here to keep me busy for the rest of my life. I knew instinctively that I didn't measure up to the standard of godliness that I was reading.

I've met a lot of churched women over the years who have varying views on these biblical passages about women. Some have developed a flinch and twitch when they hear them (often because those parts have been weaponized against them like a 1950s law bomb). In contrast, there are those who never talk about the Bible except to quote Titus 2 or 1 Peter 3; they are content to live there. And then there are some with a chip on their shoulder who just flat out refuse to allow the Bible to say what it says to women, doing feats of flexibility with the Scriptures that twist the Bible to the point that all blood flow is cut off to inconvenient passages like 1 Timothy 2:11–15 and the prohibition of women teaching men based on the order of creation.[12] Those parts just fall off for them as irrelevant or wrong.

In the English department at my college, there was the occasional lopping off of parts of literature deemed harmful to women by those doing critical gender studies. Who were these dead white guys to be telling us what good literature is, to be writing female characters for us? Why should enlightened women read such dregs, except to refute them? And for some, this has extended to God's Word. If dead white guys can be cast off, why not dead Middle Eastern guys too?

But the Bible isn't a trifle. It isn't *Gulliver's Travels* or *Great Expectations.* Its author is divine, not dead; perfect, not sinful. To read it is to be changed or judged, in some measure. We either come under it in full-stop submission, or we cast it aside as boring or harmful or stupid or nice. In unmitigated pride we may even exploit it. And God's Word isn't something indifferent; it masters us willingly now or unwillingly later.

The Whole Bible Is for Women

The God of the Bible won't be suppressed to a few select passages directed toward women. He also won't allow his daughters to cut off blood supply to the parts of the Bible we don't like very much. He demands all of himself for all of ourselves.

Thankfully, God moved me into all of his Word. Understanding myself as his daughter is no longer based on just three or four texts or on drawing out implications from narratives about women; it's informed by the whole Bible. It is informed by everything it means to be a Christian. When that is brought to bear on me, a woman, it shapes me into a godly woman, not an indistinct human. Paul instructs us all, "Let the word of Christ dwell in you richly" (Col. 3:16). Maybe the Lord is reminding you today that the whole Bible is for you, to dwell in you richly, as he reminded me those many years ago, and that the effect of bringing his whole Word to bear on *you*—a *woman*—will be to shape you into a *Christian woman*.

When Paul tells the Corinthians, "Be imitators of me, as I am of Christ" (1 Cor. 11:1), he isn't talking to men only. He's talking to all of us. This means that we don't have to knock our heads against a wall searching for obscure women in the biblical text that we can imitate, as if other women are our only designated mentors. We don't have to try to draw elaborate conclusions and applications for our lives from a brief mention in one verse tucked away in Paul's closing remarks, simply because it was about a woman. We can take that brief mention for what it is—helpful, important, instructive—but not the sum total of God's Word for us.

No Smugness toward Any Part of the Bible

So what does this mean for the parts of the Bible that pertain to women? Are we above them now? No, we aren't. Are they worth our focus, our study, our attention? Yes, they are. Imagine receiving a letter addressed to your family from an uncle. It begins, "Dear Family," and goes on for five paragraphs. The sixth paragraph starts, "To my nieces." We would give full attention to the whole letter, as some of the main points will be in the larger body. But we would give special attention to the parts written just to us. We must not elevate certain parts of the Bible over and above other parts. But God forbid we snigger in our sleeves while we put ourselves above those "silly girl" sections, having assigned them some kitschy name, and smugly disdain the women who take them seriously.

God has brought me back to those "women" sections with new eyes. Appreciative eyes. Humbled eyes. Eyes that can see them as part of the whole. They are not insignificant, nor are they to be plucked out and isolated from the rest. They are treasures; they are an integral, lovely aroma of Christ. So read good books on the Proverbs 31 woman with thankfulness. Study the women of the Old Testament. Embrace the feminine virtues as fully as you possibly can. But also read everything else. Read the commands given to all God's people. Be awed by God's work in Abraham and Moses and Joseph and David. See the types of Christ. Listen to the gospel again and again. Receive and obey it all, as the woman you are.

Women, we harm ourselves when we use the Bible as a how-to book on being a woman *only* rather than look to it to see our God and Savior, who teaches us all things. Yet to leave off the reality of being a woman, thinking we can submit to God without submitting to God's very good creational order, wars against him. Both fundamental realities joined together are the parable that defines us. We have the privilege, the freedom, the endowment of being fully Christian and fully woman.

Discussion Questions

1. How familiar are you with God's Word? Have you read the whole Bible?

2. What parts of the Bible are you most apt to camp out in? What parts do you avoid?

3. How can you begin to see the whole Bible as needful for your knowledge of God and for your growth as a Christian woman?

5

Embodied Women

And he is the head of the body, the church. He is the beginning, the firstborn from the dead, that in everything
he might be preeminent. For in him all the fullness of
God was pleased to dwell. *Colossians 1:18–19*

When I was in the doctor's office getting an ultrasound for our second child, we had the fun of finding out whether the baby was a boy
or a girl. We'd tossed around names and pondered the implications
of a boy when it came to the nursery décor and clothes, since we already had a girl. But even with all that, I couldn't have predicted the
very ridiculous thought that would come into my head as the ultrasound tech told us, "It's a boy!" I thought to myself, "Well, that's
impossible. I'm a girl. How can I have a boy growing inside of me?"
As odd as that thought was, if you're like me, you may have had a
similar notion when it comes to our new birth in Christ.

When you were reborn in Christ, what were you reborn as? The
obvious answer is, as a Christian. This is the most beautiful truth
in the world! But more specifically, were you reborn as a brand-new

you, as a woman? Or in becoming a Christian did you then transcend your physical body? What's the point of a womb or arms or feet or no Adam's apple in Christ's mission in the world? If our humanity does not transcend our gender, as we saw in chapter 4, then does our Christianity rise above our female bodies?

When we receive Christ, we die *as women*—each of us as a particular woman. We die in him, to our sin and ourselves. And when we are born again, it is not as though the doctor checks and says, "It's a girl!" with astonishment. Rather, our God knowingly announces, "That's *my* girl." And it is a double good. We do not have the same experience as Adam and Eve of being created without sin, according to God's image. We were born in Adam's sin, and from our first moment, we are a broken, marred, and distorted humanity—so much so that it cannot be patched up. We cannot go back to Eden to try to reclaim the pre-curse status to find meaning. We must go forward to Calvary; we must go forward to another garden, the garden at Gethsemane.

It is not incidental that we are reborn as women, not as men or as vague Christian humans. Our womanly bodies assigned to us by God are now Christian womanly bodies. And they have something to tell us about our calling and mission in life.

A lasting echo of the Enlightenment, strengthened by modern hubris, tells us that to know our calling, we must look within. Self-knowledge of the inner person is how we discern what we're made for. And there's an element of truth there; we can't ignore our inner life. Yet if we want to know what we're made for, we need something more fixed and unchanging than our internal selves. We need Jesus Christ, who is the same yesterday, today, and forever (Heb. 13:8), and we need to observe the bodies he has given us, created through him and for him (Col. 1:16–17).

Why are hammers heavy and flat on one side? Why do books fit in your hand so nicely? Why is the bench at a piano at just the right height and the keys of the piano sized right for fingers? Why do hoses stretch long and attach to spigots? And why are women soft, with breasts and arms and curved hips and feet and legs and a mind and a uterus and a monthly cycle? Why are grandmothers extra soft?

Is it all just a fluke? What does it matter? Perhaps you think I'm minimizing your personhood, reducing women to the sum of their parts, implying that women are no more than a baby incubator, or worse: no more than their sexuality.

We Are Not Less Than Our Bodies

But hear me out. Women are certainly more than their sexuality; we are more than a uterus or legs; we are more than softness and curves, more than even our minds, but we are not less than those things. We are not less than the bodies God has given us. Bodies matter. And these bodies will take us to our dying day or until he comes again, and then they will be made new and last forever. So God thinks pretty highly of our bodies. He's not shelving the idea.

The devastating way our society treats the calling of women's bodies is to cleverly uncover them and use them for power and money. How many daughters and sisters and mothers and friends believe their bodies to be valuable only as they are objectified or viewed with lust? Or only as they earn capital under the false banner of empowerment? Our Beyoncé-ified ideals run counter to every beat of our new-creation hearts.

The world loves women's bodies for hedonistic autonomous uses, like porn and promotion, but hates women's bodies when they do the very things they were made to do, like bring helpless children into the world and give of themselves to keep them alive. Instead of using a hammer to hammer, we polish and paint it and hang it on the wall to stare at. Instead of making music with a piano, we refuse to have it tuned and superglue the keys in place so they can't strike a chord, but, boy, do they look like they could make music, were someone ever to try them out. Instead of a woman's body bringing forth life, we make it a graveyard of unwanted children.

There are a few major exceptions to the hedonistic way of viewing our bodies that our culture heralds in an equally sinful way. They are breastfeeding, drug-free childbirth, and the promotion of "natural" bodies. This goes the other direction entirely, monumentalizing our bodies as capable of pre-curse perfection, as though we can all be fertility goddesses with the inherent ability to heal ourselves, if only we manage to follow every rule of the online gurus. Without reference to the curse of sin infecting everything, all things "natural" become innately good and holy.

With plastic surgery and an inordinate emphasis on perfect health and diet, our bodies have become something like a mausoleum that we dare not spend or use for any purposes other than the ones we decide will benefit us. So while a woman may be quite happy to test her body's limits at the gym so that she looks cute and young in a new outfit, many wouldn't dream of testing its limits in hard labor of any kind for a purpose with no personal benefit, solely for the sake of another. Even natural childbirth, which women often undertake for selfless reasons of wanting to spare their baby potential contact with drugs, is too often overrun by women undertaking it for reasons of self-actualization, badge earning, and one-upsmanship.

Christian women must understand our bodies as a part of God's unbreakable revelation to us.

Why Weaker?

A package came in the mail with the warning "Fragile: Handle with Care." We fastidiously cut open the cardboard and were disappointed to find a few broken pieces inside. If only the fast-moving conveyor belts and jostling trucks could have read this helpful label. Then they'd have known to give it its proper consideration and value.

A glass chandelier is exquisite in its fragility. We could replace it with a wooden one, sturdy and functional, which would have a certain virtue to it but would lack all the things that make a chandelier what it is: the light that twinkles off the multifaceted glass, the gentle, high chinkling of pieces as they're nudged, the suspended refinement that underscores a necessary sort of civilization. It would be a mistake to deem a chandelier worthless because it's fragile. It misses the point.

Fragility isn't a defect; it may be the defining worth of a thing.

We see a similarity in women's bodies. No, I'm not saying women are chandeliers. I'm not even saying they're fragile. Have you seen a woman in labor? But they are physically weaker than men. How is it that God calls women to "do good and do not fear anything that is frightening" (1 Pet. 3:6) in one verse, and in the next verse refers to them as a "weaker vessel" (1 Pet. 3:7)? We don't often put *fearless* and *weaker* together.

What results from being physically weaker than men? Should we feel insulted because we acknowledge this biological fact? Or could our very nature as weaker lead us to the source of our fearlessness, a powerlessness resulting in trust in the all-powerful Father?

It helps to first acknowledge that what God says through Peter is true. We *are* weaker than men. Not less intelligent. Not less human. Not incapable of reason or achievement. Not emotionally broken. Not more sinful. And not even without great strength, as the Scriptures testify. But, as relates to our physical bodies, comparatively weaker. And yet many of us are, or have been at some point, uncomfortable with this because it's inimical to the spirit of the age, and it's an offense to our pride—so much so that we might stubbornly spurn 1 Peter's verity, even as we take every precaution when walking alone in a dark alley.

Our being physically weaker by comparison—the fact that no matter how much time I spend in the gym, I'll likely never be able to overpower an average-sized man or beat him in an arm-wrestling match—is not a sign of something gone wrong. It is something to be handled with care, because in it resides exquisite beauties, abilities, and feminine strengths, like the beautiful strength of thick beveled glass.

A pregnant woman is one of the most defenseless humans on the face of the earth. She can barely rise to her feet after sinking into a comfy couch. Yet who but the weaker vessel, called woman, can grow another human inside her body?

Think of the massive strength and endurance it takes to give birth, yet it is simultaneously a vulnerable type of vigor. A woman in a marathon labor of countless hours afterward sits up in bed, even as her body begins to hemorrhage, trying to feed and care for another person. Why did God do it this way? So that we would know that, like a mother with her nursing babe, he never forgets us, even as the blood drained out of his own Son on our behalf. It's a fragile, mind-bogglingly valiant design pointing to bigger things to be honored and protected—not belittled by comparison with a man, but accurately understood by it.

It is good that God made you weaker; he's put a resplendent design in two Xs. In Lewis's *The Voyage of the Dawn Treader,* young Eustace tells Ramandu, a former star, "In our world, a star is a huge ball of flaming gas." But Ramandu replies, "Even in your world, my son, that is not what a star is, but only what it is made of."[13] We may be made of repeat chromosomes, but it amounts to so much more than the reductionism of what can be seen under a microscope.

Why Wombs and Breasts?

God gave women wombs so that babies could grow in them. Does every woman's womb grow a baby? No, and there is no lessening of womanhood in that. But wombs to grow babies is the design; that's the boggling plan. It was his idea to give those to women. And knowing that God gave that to you helps make sense of life.

If God designed our bodies to be a home to a tiny person for nine months, then that understanding will help us understand the instructions in Titus 2 or 1 Timothy 5 to work and manage the home. Why? Because he actually *made our bodies a home.* Making a home for others is how he made us—it's part of God's revelation. Women's bodies nourish life from within and without—we may bristle when it's said that a woman's place is in the kitchen, but God said something strikingly similar when he made us: our *bodies* are the kitchen, the garden, the food, the stationary home that must be sought over and over for nourishment. But it's not just for nourishment; it's also for connection and intimacy.

The threads that run between a woman and the members of her family are unique. Rochester tells Jane Eyre that it's as though a string has been tied under his left ribs connecting him to a similar knotted string in her."[14] We can relate to Rochester, because we have as many strings knotted around our hearts as friends and family members. This isn't because women are silly and sentimental; it is because we were made to hold people close together with the bond of community and love and nourishment.

Making a home for others is perhaps the most influential thing we will ever do. The weight of influence that comes in making a home, in ordering a dwelling place for others, is practically incalculable. Proverbs says the "wisest of women builds her house" (Prov. 14:1). That's one reason God gave us hands and arms—to build our house, to make a home.

I'm not saying that we all must have as many babies as we can or that our arms should lift things in perpetuity or that our legs should never stop walking. I'm simply pointing to the design and asking, *Why did God make us like this? Are we willing to accept the answer inherent in God's design and inerrant in his Word?*

The truth, of course, about God's clear design doesn't leave us without complex pains and questions. What about women who suffer with infertility or have had mastectomies or hysterectomies, or a leg amputated, or are blind, or in any way have a body that doesn't function properly?

We begin by acknowledging that's all of us at some level. Not all of us have parts missing, but all of us have a level of body dysfunction. That's what sin does: it corrupts the creation. And that doesn't make us any less a woman or our bodies any less relevant or our design any less important. A woman who cannot make a home inside her body for children can still make a home for them outside of it. She can make a place of safety and warmth for others, whether they're her children or not.

My husband, Tom, has injuries in his arms and hands. Early in our marriage he could use them very little. I did most of the physical jobs, including the care of our young children. So God gave him arms and hands, but he took the function away. God sometimes does that to his children. He gives them something such as arms, which are for a clear purpose, then he thwarts the ability. I can't tell you all the specific reasons why, except that I can say there may be hundreds of them, and one of them is to receive glory from the lack—to be shown to be enough. And even though men are made to be stronger than women and physically bear the load, it doesn't lessen a man's calling as a man when he's unable to do that. It just means that the external form of it is hindered; but the reality of manhood is not hindered in the least. Quite the opposite. When is a man as admirable as when he humbly accepts his limitations and still shoulders the load for his family in ways that are deeper than merely physical?

Our youngest son is disabled. He has a body and mind that "don't work the way they're supposed to," though we believe his body and mind work precisely the way God intends. So what does it mean for our son to live a full life as an embodied soul, whose body has something to say about his calling? It means that while his calling will remain the same—the call to live as a Christian man, God willing—how it works out will be different, because he'll be in his particular body, not someone else's.

Likewise, God has given Christian women the calling to be Christian women, even when their bodies have a womb that cannot carry babies. As Christians, we're all singing the same song, with the same goal, with our varied parts, some on melody, some on harmony and descant, and some sounding the minor note. And while the song is beautiful, it is, at times, heartbreakingly so.

The inability to bear children can be agonizing. It is a grief worth grieving. It does not make you lesser; you are loved, and, oh, how we need you. Your body is not irrelevant, nor is your womb. It points to something; it is valuable and made by God.

Sometimes the glory God gets from our lack far exceeds what he gets from our fullness. Empty wombs and broken bodies point to greater realities—not despite the sorrow that comes with them, but with the sorrow as the pointer.

Commissioned as Christ's Body

There is a great mystery in the Christian life. It is that while we each have our own body, the calling of each Christian life must be understood in the context of another's body—Christ's body. So we must look at the design of our physical body as a type of revelation from God that points us in a direction toward his intended and varying purposes for each one. Yet our body's purpose and meaning are fully and completely understood within Christ's body, the church.

The service carried out by our bodies for one another, the brothers and sisters, is our living sacrifice to God. Romans connects these two truths: our bodies are a living sacrifice to God (Rom. 12:1), and that sacrifice is understood in the context of Christ's body and the exercise of our gifts in it. "Having gifts that differ according to the grace given to us, let us use them" (Rom. 12:6)

When God said, "Be fruitful and multiply and fill the earth" (Gen. 1:28), he was commissioning us. He was telling us to fill the earth with his image, which can't happen without women's bodies. After the fall, that commission changed, and he gave us a new commission in Matthew: "Go therefore and make disciples of all nations" (Matt. 28:19). We are still to fill the earth with God's image, and that image is Christ in us. That's our calling, and it still takes our bodies to accomplish that purpose. Whether he chooses to do it by giving us children whom we nurture in the Lord, or by using us to disciple relatives, neighbors, and far away nations, our bodies matter.

This is the beauty of the new commission—it doesn't need fertile bodies to spread the good news. Shockingly, cracked and broken jars carry it better than shiny ones. Fertility and fruitfulness have been redefined in Christ's body. A woman can nourish life and build the bonds of Christian community wherever God has her, whatever her body may be like.

Our feet are meant to carry good news; our mouths are meant to tell it; our eyes are meant to see the needs; our hands are meant to stretch out and meet them. Our bodies are a living sacrifice to God, and he knows exactly what to do with them when we offer them to him. His way might not be the way we'd have planned it, but we can rest assured we aren't getting a bum deal. Whatever giftings or lack you sense in your body, it is meant to fit together with the needs and strengths of the rest of his body.

After our new birth in Christ, the way we view our bodies changes dramatically. They aren't something we use for worldly gain. We aren't trying to overcome or transcend our bodies in favor of a disembodied thought life. Biological child bearing is not the pinnacle of existence. Now, rather than finding meaning in what our bodies can achieve or trying to prop them up for as long as we can, we spend them for the sake of Christ's body. Instead of wasting our lives on a form of asceticism that desires body perfection, so our bodies *look* really young and able, we take the glory of Christ within our perishable, mortal bodies and feed him to hungry children—biological or not. We make a home for the nations by calling them to be a part of the imperishable, immortal body of Christ.

Discussion Questions

1. When you think of your body's uses or potential uses (like having strong arms for lifting, legs for walking, a womb for bearing a baby, etc.), have you ever considered that your body is a type of revelation from God—a way that he is communicating with you what you were made for?

2. How do you reconcile the good design of what our bodies are made for with the reality that our bodies don't work properly some of the time or can't be used for their intended purpose?

3. Have you considered the deeper, spiritual reality that your physical body points to—the body of Christ? How can you participate in that body—the church—in fullness, even when you can't participate fully with your physical body in all the ways it was designed to work?

6

(A)Typical Women

Have this mind among yourselves, which is yours in
Christ Jesus, who, though he was in the form of God,
did not count equality with God a thing to be grasped.
Philippians 2:5–6

"I guess I'm not a typical woman," I heard a woman say. She spoke
of her love for sports and her lack of emotion, as she made this
(ironically typical) confession. This got me thinking: how many
of us would call ourselves typical women? What do we mean by it?
And is being typical a good thing?

In my conversations with ladies of many ages, I've noticed that
we have varying understandings of what a typical woman is, but
few of us think of ourselves as a typical woman. Start a conversation with a woman in your church, ask her all about herself, find
out her life story, and usually you will hit a point where she tells
you that she doesn't or didn't feel like a typical woman. We may not
think of ourselves as special or unique, but many of us have had the
experience of feeling like we didn't quite fit the mold.

Maybe you didn't like to play with dolls as a child, or maybe you love wielding power tools. Perhaps you are really awkward around children, or you despise shopping or love woodworking. Some have a nagging feeling of incompetence as a mom or have nonexistent cooking skills or were considered a tomboy or the only female math major in college. I know many women whose husbands talk more than they do, or they have a hard time connecting with other women, or a hundred other ways women don't feel like they are quite the typical woman—depending on what their view of *typical* is.

Some are happy to be different from the perceived norm—and proud—as if the closer they get to what is regarded as masculine, the more powerful or respected they will be. Their view of womanhood is narrow and somewhat pathetic, so it makes sense that they'd want to distance themselves from it. Others are sad, and even ashamed, that no one taught them what womanhood was supposed to look like, and now they fumble around in the dark trying to figure it out.

Anything but Typical

As Christians who have the benefit of God's own revelation of the truth in the Bible to help us navigate this world, along with the benefit of the creation itself to clue us in on God's design, we need not fixate on what our society calls "typical." The goal of a Christian woman isn't to be typical. Especially if what *typical* means is an overly made-up, hyper-feminine, wilts-at-the-first-sign-of-hardwork, check-brain-at-the-door type of woman. Where is that in the Bible? Thankfully, fainting couches and Southern belles aren't mentioned either. Rather, we live our life in Christ and pursue holiness, and that is anything but typical.

When, as a child, I watched my mom, a farmer's daughter, use the chainsaw to take down dead branches and load them into the trailer to haul to the brush pile, I was learning about being a woman. When I saw her prepare our home for countless guests and food for countless mouths, I was learning about being a woman. When I heard her discuss the Bible with dozens in our living room every Tuesday night, I was learning about being a woman, because she was a woman doing those things. And thankfully, for me, she was more—she was a Christian woman.

When we read the narratives of godly women in Scripture, the same thing is happening—we have the advantage of observation, of watching particular women face particular situations. We watch the Hebrew midwives fear God more than Pharaoh and, in so doing, save the Hebrew sons (Ex. 1:15–21). We see Rahab earnestly bind herself to Yahweh, putting her life on the line for his people (Joshua 2; 6:17–25), and Sarah believe that God would provide a son against all odds (Heb. 11:31), and teenage Mary magnify the Lord in the strangest of circumstances (Luke 1:46–55), and Prisca risk her neck for Paul (Rom. 16:3–4).

In all these we learn about being women, not as a handbook of what we must do with our lives but as varied examples of God-fearing women through the ages. And we learn that far from being typical, we must be faithful women in the life and circumstances he has given us.

Putting Feelings in Their Place

I wonder if we can all agree that how we *feel* about being a woman doesn't have any bearing on what we are. We may feel like we don't fit the mold, but God calls us to live in a way that shatters the world's expectations. So in our misfit feelings, he has actually given us a gift. Our misfit feelings don't change reality. We are women. When we act, when we do whatever it is we do, we do so as women, and we become a living narrative that models womanhood to those around us, for good or ill.

As Christian women, we are telling people what God is like. Not because God is a woman, but because we bear his image, are clothed in Christ, and have his Spirit at work in us. We are his representatives—as women. We tell a story with all we say and do about who God is. That God made you a woman is an essential part of the story he is telling about himself.

So what does your life as a unique woman tell the people around you about God? When we walk in holiness with our God-ordained peculiarities, in his lovingly appointed circumstances, we tell the world the truth about God. When we indulge in sinful proclivities, we distort the truth about him. And perhaps the most important, powerful thing we tell the people around us, living as Christian women, is that we are not stuck in sin.

We are never powerless in our sin, because the same power that raised Jesus from the dead is at work in us to make us new. The story we tell when we repent and turn is the gospel story. It is the truest thing we can say with our lives.

Don't Be Typical

The other gracious thing God has done is make a whole body to show forth his glory. I'm so thankful that my kids have Christian women to learn from other than me—women whose lives are marked by obedience to God. Through them they see faithful women with skills in management and organization, women navigating disability, women who teach science and piano, women who enjoy ironing and are excellent meal planners and dearly love to laugh. They are atypical because in whatever they do, they do so to God's glory—and that is rare indeed.

When I reflect on the women and men who have had the most acute and lasting influence on my life, it isn't their disarming humor and relatable stories that impact me. In many cases, I couldn't relate to their experiences at all. I can't relate to Betsy Ten Boom's contentment in a concentration camp or Elisabeth Elliot's weathering the loss of a murdered husband while ministering to the ones who murdered him or even John Piper's forsaking a television. And that lack of "typicality"—the fact that I can't relate—is precisely what calls me away from the longing to be normal or relatable or typical and into a greater desire for holiness and a greater desire for the God who empowers such joyful holiness. In their set-apartness, they beckon me to Christ, the sympathetic High Priest, who is the most atypical of all.

So be encouraged and truly liberated, all you atypical women. God doesn't ask you to be typical. He calls you to be his. He calls for unequivocal submission and loyalty to himself, and this requirement is the most loving thing he could command of you. A life of obedience to God is the riskiest kind of life that has ever been truly safe. And as he commands our submission to him and his Book and his design, he simultaneously enables it through the limitless power of his saving Son.

Discussion Questions

1. Are there ways that you feel like a misfit as a woman?

2. Can feeling like an atypical, misfit woman change what you actually are? Who decides what you are? Why is this good news for us?

3. How do you think God might want to use your misfit feelings to honor and glorify himself? How might those feelings actually be a gift to your growth in godliness?

PART 2

WOMEN IN ALL WE DO—IN CHRIST

. . . so as to walk in a manner worthy of the Lord, fully pleasing to him: bearing fruit in every good work and increasing in the knowledge of God. *Colossians 1:10*

7

Transforming Women

And we all, with unveiled face [through Christ], beholding the glory of the Lord, are being transformed into the
same image from one degree of glory to another. For this
comes from the Lord who is the Spirit. *2 Corinthians 3:18*

Have you ever heard a little child babble in seemingly incoherent
speech with a look of intelligence and satisfaction as you struggle
to understand a single syllable coming from her tiny mouth? If
you're lucky, that little one's mother is nearby and inexplicably
able to translate and transform the babble into sentences. All the
sudden "ya-ya wa wa-wa" is shown for what it is: "Elianna wants
water." Duh. Clearly the child is destined for greatness. Or at least
the mom has a bright future in toddler-ese.

This ability to take raw materials and rudimentary stuff and
turn it into more, in other words, to glorify it, is a sometimes forgotten part of being a Christian woman. You may wonder why I
place this emphasis on *women* being transformative. Aren't men
transformative? Yes. But I'll leave that to someone else to write

about. I emphasize it because I see it in the Scriptures and in God's creation called "woman."

A woman is to be compared to a crown on the head of her husband (Prov. 12:4). This is not because she's merely decorative, but because she is the thing that makes her good man great. She transforms a promising bachelor into a purposeful, respected husband. He gives his seed and by some miracle and mystery, God has designed her body to nurture and grow a new person.[15]

Womanhood Is a Prism

A woman is a prism that takes in light and turns it into an array of greater, fuller glory so that others now see the rainbow that was contained in the beam. She constantly radiates reminders of God's faithfulness. She reads the black-and-white pages of the Word of God and takes on the task of living them out in vibrant hues for her children, her neighbors, and the world to see. When the Bible commands feeding, nourishing, training, and love, a godly woman sets to the task, better-ifying and beautifying everything around her.

Perhaps the most poignant vision we have of this transforming woman is in the oft-dreaded Proverbs 31 woman par excellence. That brief section of Scripture from verses 10 to 31 has inspired countless pages, both idolizing it and tearing it down. I have found myself on opposite sides of it, both looking to it for everything and then, consequently, almost nothing. Whole articles are spent explaining why no woman should attempt to be a Proverbs 31 woman, how we aren't *meant* to be her, that she is a mythical figure, the personification of wisdom, and most importantly, we are told, *do not try this at home!* Move along, folks, nothing to see here.

Assuming that she is not a real person but a figurative example and a composite of many virtuous women, and assuming she is the personification of wisdom and in many ways unattainable, doesn't she still have something to teach us? Even as we maintain that we cannot *be* her—considering that for most of us, planting a vineyard is simply out of the question (v. 16)—is she not given to us as a worthy example in principle? And even if we hold that *only Jesus* is able to fulfill all the qualities she exudes, is it not true for those of us clothed in Christ and his righteousness that we are to imitate him—he who is perfect in every way? At the very least, the Scriptures seem to maintain that we should at least revere the virtues she represents, not scorn the passage.

Why did God choose to make this picture of wisdom a woman? Is it a mere literary device that ought to be deconstructed? Ought not men also imitate her? Well, sure, except for the part about her being a *wife* and all. It may be a literary device, but that doesn't make it *less* applicable to women by the acknowledgment that men have much to gain from it as well. It adds meaning; it doesn't subtract from it. So, yes, men have much to learn from her. Yet women will have a more concrete and tangible relationship with the concept of being a wife, as they actually have the potential to live that out.

We've gotten so bent out of shape about this excellent woman that men are chastised for desiring a Proverbs 31 woman (*No such woman exists! Lower your standards, man! Don't expect any such goodness from me!*) and simultaneously told that it was likely a song sons were to memorize in praise of their (future?) wives. Hmm. But if no woman really is meant to be like her, then wouldn't it be false flattery to teach sons to sing such a song? Or worse, a not so subtle hint of all that his wife should be, but isn't? We don't have to wonder how that would go over.

A New Heart for Proverbs 31

When we turn Proverbs 31 into a heavy burden, it's no wonder we're eager to cast it off. But like all of God's ideals that we cannot meet, we rest in the One who met them for us. We do not operate as those earning our salvation by becoming the excellent wife. We come broken, sick, wandering, and anything but excellent. It is God who transforms us. It is God who does the mighty, deep, and wonderful renewal. And our transforming is only ever born from that. A heart that desires to be like the representative woman from Proverbs 31 or *any* holy woman of the Scriptures is itself a testament to transformation—none of us desires that on our own. None of us desires wisdom or holiness apart from God working a miracle in our heart.

So, if you feel something less than love and admiration for the portrait God saw fit to give us in Proverbs 31 (or *any* part of God's perfect Word), the place to start is a new heart, and only God can supply it. If Proverbs 31 makes you feel like someone loaded giant bags of luggage on your back, it is time to lay those down at the cross. And once we've been transformed, we will begin to see the beauty of the myriad ways God invites us to transform actual tangible things around us and make them better for his glory.

The ideal woman will no longer be a threat or a requirement but inspiring and glorious as we observe that everything she touches, she improves to yield a return. We will see this as freedom, not bondage. Don't we want that good for the people around us? Don't we desire to be wise and transformative and more like Christ? God's design outlined in the Scriptures is a vision for womanhood that is not just right and to be obeyed; it is experientially preferable to all the world has to offer. And it doesn't apply just to those who are married or mothers. Single women of any age are meant for full transformative womanhood. They are meant to be Christian women in the deepest sense, that is, spiritually nurturing and growing all God has given them.

Spent for Glory

Unfortunately, being an agent of transformation or influence is not confined to betterment. Worldliness also transforms—sin transforms. When we walk in sin, we take good things and sour them. Our child wakes up cheerfully, and we transform that cheerfulness into gloom as we rail about the mess that didn't get picked up. Our husband comes home from work eager to see us, and we make him sorry he ever had such a thought as we snap and gripe about our day. Our friend is excited to share her good news, and we turn it into an occasion for envy, comparison, and anger. We may laugh at the old saying, "When mama ain't happy, ain't nobody happy," but it is a testament to the truth that we transform the very air our people breathe, for good or ill.

What a different kind of transforming happens for the woman who is in Christ. In this transformative role, whether single or married, a woman mimics her Savior. Like him, she submits to God's will, and, also like him, God uses her to take what was useless on its own and shape it into glory: dirty things clean; chaos turned to order; an empty kitchen overflowing with life and food; a lonely apartment changed by a simple open door and warm welcome as women eagerly gather to study God's Word; children in want of knowledge and truth and a mother eager to teach; a man in need of help and counsel and a woman equipped to give it.

God has made us for glory—not glory that terminates on us, but glory that permeates everything given to us and points in all things to Christ, who is the radiance of the glory of God, the Savior and ultimate transforming One. And as we behold him—his perfection, his saving work, his glorious face—we are changed from one degree of glory to another (2 Cor. 3:18).

Discussion Questions

1. How has the gospel of Jesus Christ transformed your life?

2. Where did this transformation begin, and how much of your life do you think God wants to transform?

3. How do you think God wants to use Christ in you as an agent of transformation in the lives of those around you? How can you set about this task physically and spiritually?

8

Single Women

... that their hearts may be encouraged, being knit together in love, to reach all the riches of full assurance
of understanding and the knowledge of God's mystery,
which is Christ, in whom are hidden all the treasures of
wisdom and knowledge. *Colossians 2:2–3*

My memories of singleness are potent but few. Unlike many, I was
engaged at twenty and married before I finished college. Still, I remember singleness. I remember the thrill and horror of dating. Singleness is more common, more accepted, more in vogue than it has
been for quite some time, at least from an outsider's perspective.
I, for one, feel like cheering when I see single women who aren't
pining away or waiting for their life to begin with the entrance of
the mythical man who will fulfill all their deepest longings. There
is a man able to satisfy our longings, but he isn't mythical, and he
arrived over two thousand years ago.

But for all that, there are still many women living with unwanted singleness. And none of us was made to live alone. In the

garden of Eden, God remedied the problem of aloneness by creating Eve for Adam. If it's true that man and woman complete each other, then who completes the single person?

You Complete Me?

Our instinct for Sunday-school answers has us ready to say, "Jesus!" But is that right? Is Jesus just the missing puzzle piece to an otherwise whole person? No. Jesus doesn't complete the incomplete. He utterly overcomes and swallows us up in himself—in his death and resurrection. We are made new and whole in Christ, not merely completed by him. So who does complete the single person?

I may be an unlikely candidate to answer the question, but I have a perspective to offer. I have had the humbling privilege of being loved, taught, discipled, and mothered by singles, and I want to tell the stories. What I'm most used to hearing regarding married people and single people is that families should make singles part of their lives—fold them in. I agree! But I also want to encourage married women and mothers to come under the mentorship and wisdom of singles, not to believe the lie that singles aren't qualified as counselors and mentors because they lack marital experience. I want to encourage married women to give the single person the right to speak into their lives, on any subject, even marriage and parenting.

Not long after my husband and I started having children, I, along with a few other young moms, was invited to the home of a woman of our church named Joyce. As I entered, I noticed how lovely and orderly everything was, how wonderful her food smelled, how the table was set. As Joyce introduced herself, and everyone settled in for a little chatter, my first impression was that she was clearly a woman I could learn a lot from. She was kind, warm, comfortable with people, and just what you'd want a mother or aunt or grandmother to be.

Later in our visit, I found myself telling Joyce about a parenting difficulty I was having. She responded, "I've never had children, so I don't know if this is helpful, but here's what I've observed with my nieces and nephews . . ." To my shame, this surprised me. Even more so, to find out later that she had never been married. I hadn't considered the possibility that the woman eager to take some green moms under her wing would be single. She went on to give me some stellar Christ-honoring parenting advice that I took to the bank. I also got some good recipes out of the deal.

A few years ago, I had the joy of being in a Bible study discussion group with Joyce. I gave thanks over and over as her gentle wisdom and thorough knowledge of the Word helped keep our group on course, with our eyes fixed on Christ.

Emily is ten years younger than I am, and I first got to know her when I started cold-calling families from our church directory in a desperate attempt to find babysitters for the mass of children in our small group. She was in high school at the time, and she, along with her younger sisters, agreed to help immediately. They faithfully served our small group for the next six years. A few years later, Emily started college, and I was in over my head with adding children to our family, homeschooling, and plain ol' life. I asked her if she'd be interested in coming weekly to help me out. Again, her commitment to the job was unlike what you might expect from a young person. She showed up and worked hard. She shared the knowledge, tips, and habits she'd learned from her mom, which were made all the more poignant when her mom passed away from cancer during her freshman year at college. I learned a lot from Emily, such as a better way to match socks and that organizing can be simple. But mostly I learned about faithfulness—faithfulness to commitments and faithfulness to God in the darkest times.

My Aunt Julie has always been an integral part of my life. From living with us briefly when I was growing up, to being a fixture in my kids' lives today, her lifelong singleness has been a gift to us.

I don't say that to minimize the difficulty of it. Yet it remains a fact that her singleness coupled with her willingness to love us, warts and all, and take us under her wing and make us her own, is a type of auntly mothering that is as precious as it is unique. When I watch my four-year-old son's face light up at the sight of her or see the older kids sprint to invade the privacy of her room, I'm thankful. I've learned about good parenting and happy marriages from her, as she's shared about her folks—my grandparents, who have passed away—and other examples she had the privilege of seeing close-up.

We Need One Another

Time fails me to tell of Char, whose devotion to God and his people and the unreached around the world was a force that could topple kings and nations; or Great Aunt Ola, who at one hundred years old still would pray before a meal in Swedish and never met a child who didn't qualify as one of her "peanuts"; or Sue, a single mom who taught me how to pray and to love others when I was a pesky teenager; or Lindsey, who expected more of our special-needs son than I would have and uses her skills as a physical therapist to do good. The faithful witness and example of these single women is beautiful. And, married ladies, we have a lot to learn from these sisters.

Single women are equipped to mother in the practical, real-life-training ways and to mother in the directly spiritual-discipleship ways. The line between the two is not sharp; as a matter of fact, there is no line between the two—they spill over and encompass each other.

So in answer to the question, "Who completes me?" I hope single women don't find it a sad consolation when the rest of the body of Christ replies, "I do." And you complete us too. The married cannot say to the single, "I have no need of you." The single cannot say to the married, "I have no need of you" (1 Cor. 12:21).

Look around at the believers in your local church. They are in Christ, and so are you. You need them. *And they need you* and all that you have to offer, more than you may realize, for we are all members of one another (Rom. 12:5).

The Gift of Singleness?

If I could impress one thing into the hearts of women who are single against their will, it would be this: there are things God is giving you that come only through your singleness. I never would have thought to ask for a disabled child. I know there are people out there who do, who have a sense of calling to disability. But I really just wanted everyone to be healthy and whole, the way I envisioned things.

What I failed to see was that in being denied one thing (a healthy, able child), I was being given many other things. In being denied a child with normal muscle tone and abilities, I have been given the ability to strengthen my muscles for him. In being denied a child that could connect with me much in the first year, I was given the ability to connect with many parents and others who were hurting and in a hard spot. In being denied a child who can talk like his peers, I've been given words that are hard won, both his and mine, that communicate more deeply than I would have dreamed.

Likewise, if your singleness is unwanted, it's true that you are being denied something—a marriage relationship with a man. But you are being given things too, things that uniquely accompany what you're being denied. You don't have a husband to talk to or with whom to give and receive counsel, but you've been given a deeper dependence on our eternal groom—Jesus Christ, who always leads you on straight paths. And you've been given brothers and sisters in great measure from whom to give and receive. You may have been denied biological children, but there is no childlessness in the new covenant. You have been given children beyond counting in Christ to love, nurture, and disciple, as Paul and Jesus did. As Elisabeth Elliot reminds us, "We do not choose our gifts, remember?"[16]

You don't have the opportunity to point to Christ and his church in the earthly relationship of marriage, but you have the opportunity to show the sufficiency of Christ while you wait for something much better than the picture—the real consummation to come. God is tailor-making gifts for you that come precisely as the result of what has been withheld. You'll miss them if you're fixated on the one he has denied you.

He has given you himself, dear sister. Show us, show us all—married and single—that he is enough.

Discussion Questions

1. In 1 Corinthians 7 Paul says that singleness is a gift, just as marriage is. What is your view of singleness? Do you agree with what God's Word says about it?

2. If you are single, how can you invest deeply in the life of your church and the individual members of it?

3. If you are married, how can you fold singles into your life and look for ways not only to encourage them but to learn from them?

9

Married Women

And whatever you do, in word or deed, do everything in the name of the Lord Jesus, giving thanks to God the Father through him. Wives, submit to your husbands, as is fitting in the Lord. Husbands, love your wives, and do not be harsh with them. *Colossians 3:17–19*

Christ is the head of the church, his body, and is himself its Savior. *Ephesians 5:23*

Wading into people's marriages is as difficult as wading into their singleness. Singleness is hard because I'm not living that reality; marriage is hard because I am. My hesitation comes from the complex nature of marriage. I'm writing to you, just one person, but marriage is made up of two people who have become one flesh. So when I talk to a married woman, I'm talking to a full, complete person who has had her very self merged with another person. It makes the conversation more than a little bit variable.

Each person is unique, but when you multiply the uniqueness by marriage, the complexity increases and so does the foolishness of people who try to make their own marriage the standard for all other marriages. You need to know how to walk *in Christ* as a woman in *your* marriage, not mine.

If you used my marriage as a template, it would likely let you down, simply because it won't line up with your experience. My husband is a kind man. He enjoys conversation and often seeks my input on anything from his business to parenting to what shirt goes with what pants. He's creative and musical and responsible and wicked smart and keeps track of details. We enjoy singing and worshiping the Lord together. He's my number-one encourager when it comes to writing projects or teaching women at church. He's deeply invested in our family's flourishing. He's also a sinner, just like his wife.

We've had hard years and easier ones. We've lived through chronic health problems, starting a business with no income, miscarriage, moves, adding five children to our family, disability in our youngest son, many nights in the hospital, years of not enough sleep, tube feeding, and over three years of near daily vomit. We've also lived through the kind of happiness and joy and laughter that is impossible to fit on this page.

Chances are, I just described a husband and a marriage that differs from yours. And chances are that submission to my Tom looks different from the submission you offer to your husband—and that is how it should be. When Tom lives with me in an understanding way and loves and cherishes me, as he's commanded to, it is going to look different from how another man does that for his wife. I'm different from other women, just as my husband is different from other men.

Yet in a book about Christian women that includes a chapter on marriage, submission must be addressed. It is the elephant in the room for anyone with even a bit of familiarity with the Bible's teaching. But before we look at submission in marriage, I want us to understand submission as the whole of the Christian life, for both men and women, married and single. Why? Because submission is a necessity if we want the name "Christian." It isn't first a necessity because we're women but because we're Christians. Christ's submission to his Father while he walked on this earth was breathtaking, all-encompassing, humble, and completely beautiful.

Philippians 2 says that Jesus did not count equality with God a thing to be grasped, but made himself nothing, taking the form of a servant, and became obedient to death, even death on a cross (Phil. 2:6–8). And it is to this incredible standard that all Christians are called—this humility, this service, this obedience, and this death. When we are in Christ, his path is our path.

Submission That Fits

What is submission? What does it even mean? Is it simply obedience? There is some similarity. But I think a better way to describe it is to say that submission is willingly placing yourself under the authority of another. Christ willingly placed himself under his Father's authority when he said, "My Father, if it be possible, let this cup pass from me; nevertheless, not as I will, but as you will" (Matt. 26:39). Likewise, *every* Christian is willingly under authority, both God's authority and other Christians' authority.

Men and women are under the authority of their fellow believers and, in particular, their church's leaders. Church leaders are accountable to and, in some ways, under the authority of the rest of the church and in particular their fellow leaders. All Christians are under the authority of God and God's Word. While there is some circularity to it, there is also an ordering. The main point is that because we are in Christ, we participate in his humility, his trust, his obedience, and his overall posture of submission.

Metaphors can get us in trouble with a subject as fraught as this one, because there are always those who want to stretch them too far or make them absolute rather than use them as a simple picture that can illumine. With that caveat, gardening has given me insight into marital submission. Putting seeds in the ground, watching them spring up and bend this way and that, has taught me something. We love to plant sunflowers for their showy brilliance, but I especially love the bending and stretching they do to accommodate the sun's rays. The sunflower needs sun, so it gladly sways this way and that, turning its face wherever the sun shines. In so doing, it assures its own growth.

In a healthy marriage, a man provides for and loves his wife the way the sun provides for and gives to the sunflower. It is no terrible burden to bend this way and that in order to receive its rays. It is no awful doormat experience to follow the sun's position in the sky. In truth, this is precisely what the church is called to in its relationship to Christ—he is our Morning Star. But marital submission is a comparison, not an exact replication. Husbands are not Christ, nor are they a flaming ball of fire in the sky. We do not need husbands like we need Christ. But the comparisons help us know what we *ought to be like.* According to Ephesians 5, wives are called to be like the church, submitting to or following their husbands.

In the letter to the Colossians, Paul reminds wives to submit to their husbands "as is fitting in the Lord" (Col. 3:18). In other words, you are in the Lord! Submission is fitting for you! Why is submission fitting in the Lord? Because in the Lord submission to our husband is done by faith in Christ and is, therefore, holy; it is a beautiful picture of how the church responds to the good authority of Christ. When I submit to Tom, I am not declaring Tom to be perfectly deserving of it, or a perfect leader; I'm declaring Jesus to be perfectly deserving of it and a perfect leader. I'm declaring that I trust Christ in Tom and Christ in me. That's what it means to submit in the Lord. But when we are not in the Lord and acting by faith, submission may quickly be distorted into a thousand perverse evils.

When husbands are Christlike, treating wives with the same care they would their own body, without harshness, it's not unusual to find remarkably healthy, happy wives blossoming very much like a brilliant sunflower. But don't think a good husband ensures flourishing. He doesn't have that much power. And don't think that a woman can't flourish apart from a good man. She can and she does. That's because she has more than the metaphor—she has her Savior, the true Morning Star.

Forced Submission?

If I noticed that one of my sunflowers wasn't following the sun's position in the sky, taking my hand to force its direction would be detrimental. The sunflower would break off. Similarly, when submission is forced upon someone from the outside, it is not submission; it is coercion.

People in a position of authority who coerce those under their authority prove their actual lack of authority. This is because the nature of authority is also one of Christlikeness. This is the unbelievable reality! Both submission and authority are found in Christ, and for people in positions of submission or authority we look to Christ as our guide. In Christ's authority over his disciples he commanded them, "Follow me!" But he didn't drag them kicking and screaming to come to him. He showed them a better way; he washed their feet. His authority was proven by all who *willingly* followed, *willingly* obeyed, and *willingly* learned from him. And for those who refused to follow and rejected him, his refusal to physically or manipulatively force them to do so was also a testament to his true greatness.

No one receives Christ while simultaneously refusing him. We all come willingly; we are wooed by the unmatched love shown at the cross and the forgiveness offered there. It's there that we lay ourselves down and offer ourselves up. It's a willing offering of our lives. The willingness doesn't change the fact that it is a requirement. We all *must* submit to God. The refusal to do so will result in eternal torment. Likewise for married women, submission to our husband is commanded by God. But it can only be given willingly, once we have eyes to see and ears to hear all that God's loving design requires of us.

Where Does Your Deepest Loyalty Lie?

In a good marriage, with normal ups and downs, submission is no more a restriction or burden than receiving love is a restriction or burden. But what if you don't have a good marriage? Some marriages are hard because of difficult circumstances. But in some marriages, either the husband or the wife or both are so tangled with sin that the marriage can't thrive. If you find yourself in this type of circumstance, one where your husband is tangled in sin, you must get some things straight about the kind of woman you must be, if you are to be a Christian woman.

Our moral agency as women is in no way lessened by our submission. Submission to our husband is never meant to be submission to sin. Every now and then, I hear a view of submission in marriage that is so encompassing that it would even allow for women to submit to and become a participant in sinfulness. I wish this didn't have to be said, but, women, you are accountable to God for every deed done while you live in your body (2 Cor. 5:10; Heb. 4:13). We do not get to hide behind our husband, simply because he initiated the sin. Your participation is yours.

Our moral agency does not get a certificate of transfer from us to them when we marry, as though our brains and our biblical understanding of right and wrong aren't needed anymore. Wives, God has given you your own brain because he wants you to use it—not half-heartedly but fully. You are meant to *help*, not affirm his sin or participate in it.

When we willingly participate in sin under the guise of biblical submission, we make a mockery of God's holy design. A submissive spirit, in the truest sense, is willing and able to say *no* to evil.

If your husband wants to watch a movie that is filled with sexual inappropriateness, you must not watch it. If your husband wants to go out drinking and shirk the responsibility of children and home in favor of an evening of drunkenness, you must not go with him. If your husband requires you to forsake the fellowship of believers and the training of your children in the Lord, you must stand firmly on Christ your solid rock. If he wants you to stay silent while he beguiles and lies to your family, your church, and the world, you must be a woman of the truth. You must obey God rather than man.

When you come before the judgment seat of God, you will be held responsible for your sin—even the sin that he urged you to join. Don't get me wrong—he'll be held to account in fullness—but God gave *you* a new heart, eyes that see and ears that hear, and he put his Spirit in you. He doesn't intend for you to now close your eyes and ears or harden your heart to his Word. Do not disregard your conscience and the Spirit's voice in favor of a wayward husband's.

You must know the one to whom your deepest loyalty is owed. You must know *who* bought you at a great price, and it is not your husband; it is God. Therefore, honor God above all. Submit to your husband inasmuch as so doing is submitting to God. Truly love your husband by living a life of holiness that shines the light of Christ in the dark places. When there is a contradiction between God and your husband, and lines are drawn in the sand, you must know where you stand before it's looking you in the face.

One thing I know for sure: God makes a way for us to obey him, whether it's through submitting to our husband as is fitting in the Lord, or exercising a deeper submission to the Lord that may put us out of step with a wayward husband. He will make a way for you by the blood of his Son. You're his daughter. He loves you.

Easing Burdens, Not Piling On

For those of us in healthy marriages, we can help ease the burden of those trying to obey God in the midst of a strained marriage by refusing to act like wives have it in their power to single-handedly save and change their husbands. We can refuse to distort the words of Peter in 1 Peter 3:1–2: "Likewise, wives, be subject to your own husbands, so that even if some do not obey the word, they may be won without a word by the conduct of their wives, when they see your respectful and pure conduct."

I've seen this good admonition for wives to be pure and respectful toward disobedient husbands twisted into a heavy burden so that *wives* actually become the mediator between their husbands and God. I've even seen it used to justify why it would be okay for a wife to submit to something sinful. But there is only one mediator between God and man, and that is the Lord Jesus Christ (1 Tim. 2:5). And Peter's admonition is protecting women from participating in the disobedience of their husband. It's reminding them that their conduct stands out because it is holy—*pure* and respectful. Their conduct doesn't save their husbands though. It simply has the *potential* (not a guarantee) to win them by pointing them to the source of their purity—Jesus.

Oppression in marriage is something I don't want to leave unaddressed.[17] It usually, but not always, involves a man dominating his wife, either physically or with other methods of sinful control. The reason I say it's usually men who abuse or oppress women is that statistics bear it out, but our Bibles do also.[18] Because women are physically weaker, it makes sense that a dynamic exists where a male can more easily do harm to a female than vice versa. This gives us an understanding of why the Bible requires elders in the church to be gentle (1 Tim. 3:3) and husbands to nourish and cherish their wives as they do their own bodies (Eph. 5:28–29). This doesn't mean that because women are physically weaker, they are always victims.

Wives can sin against their husbands and entice them to sin and go after idols, as the Bible gives us ample testimony. What it does mean is that the curse is real. Rather than men and women living in harmony on mission together, we will see women being ruled over by their husbands, just as we were told in Genesis 3:16. Thankfully, the curse is being unwound and undone by Christ. He shows us a different way—one where husbands love their wives rather than rule them (Eph. 5:25).

If you are in an oppressive marriage, I urge you to go to trusted Christians in your church.[19] Our marriages are not private relationships—they are subject to the accountability of our local churches. You are part of a family, an actual body that is Christ's, and that body needs to know if one of its members is wounded. It needs to know if one part of the body has hurt or controlled another part. Balms need to be applied and infections rooted out.

So for both the woman in a thriving marriage and the woman in a hard one, the call is the same, but the earthly outcome of your marriage might not be. Walk with Christ through *your* marriage to *your* husband, not mine and not the man you thought you married.

Discussion Questions

1. In Ephesians God tells us through Paul that marriage is a picture of Christ and the church, with the wife likened to the church and the husband likened to Christ. Have you ever accidentally reversed that metaphor, thinking that Christ and the church is a picture of earthly marriage? How would getting it backward distort things?

2. Have you, whether single or married, embraced submission as a fundamental part of the Christian life? Wives, do you willingly submit to your husband as an expression of your submission to God?

3. How does the Bible help us to think rightly about abusive situations and submission to sin? Who is to have our ultimate allegiance?

10

Mothering Women

The grace of our Lord overflowed for me with the faith
and love that are in Christ Jesus. *1 Timothy 1:14*

If God gives you children, you can be assured he's called you to it. It is
no accident. This calling of motherhood is one not of broad spread-
ing but of deep rootedness. It is the call that passes the baton of faith
not just side to side or peer to peer but down through time, entrust-
ing it to another generation. It is also a call of bottomless loyalty to
the people closest to us. We spend ourselves for our children in a way
that we don't for others. They hold priority in our lives, because they,
like us with our heavenly Father, are utterly needful of us.

One of a mother's most difficult—nay, impossible, apart from
God's help—tasks is weaning her children and transferring their
source of life and comfort and home to another—to God. That is
the goal of every Christian mother. In all her loving and comfort-
ing and making home, she simply is a pointer to a better home, a
lasting one, one where she already has one foot in the door and by
her goodness is testifying to the eternal goodness.

Christian mothers are declared good because of Jesus. When God saved us, he gave us his perfectly good Son, and now that we have Jesus, we have goodness! When Jesus ascended into heaven, he left the Holy Spirit with us, to dwell in us. That *goodness* is a fruit of the Spirit seems forgotten by so many of us as we joke about our badness or lament in self-pity about it to anyone who will listen (Gal. 5:22). We'd rather celebrate our failures as a need for more grace than to do as the psalmist instructed:

> Trust in the LORD and do good.
>> Dwell in the land and befriend faithfulness. (Ps. 37:3)

And in what seems like willful misunderstanding, the claim to goodness is often immediately rebuffed as works righteousness. But it's quite the opposite. It's the refusal to continue in sin so that grace may abound. Our feet-on-the-ground, dirt-under-the-fingernails good work is evidence of the finished work of Christ, not earning of our salvation.

God Answers the Unasked Questions

When God gives us children, he answers a lot of questions in our lives—even ones we may not have thought to ask. Questions like: What should I do with my life? How much sleep do I need? What's it like to give up my body for someone? How selfish am I, *really*? Do I trust my husband as a father? How weird am I about food? What strong opinions do I have about clothing? Sleepovers? What are my views on education? Extracurricular activities?

Being a mom brings it all to the surface; it often reveals a more truthful version of ourselves, not because we were previously being untruthful but because we are now shaping a life not only for ourselves but for someone else. We are making decisions every day that can and often will impact another person's entire existence. This pressure to make sure we don't mess up our child's life is pretty intense. It creates some heat that tends to wear us down to the nubs of what we really believe about God, ourselves, and the world.

To take the pressure off, some turn to a stream of constant uplifting messages about motherhood. All encouragement, all the time. In this endless propping up, there are no bad moms. Every mom is imbued with sainthood the moment her motherly state is attained. Also in this maternal mirage, moms are the sole proprietors of hard work and sacrifice. I once heard a pastor say that it was impossible for a mom of littles to be lazy, because of the constancy of the young ones' needs. Perhaps it was true of all the women in his life; I don't question his sincerity. But it always stuck with me because I knew it wasn't really true. It *is* possible for moms of littles to be lazy. It *is* possible for moms to be bad moms. I need look no further than myself for supporting data.

We may be doing more work as a lazy mom than we did as an A student, but that's like comparing riding a bike on the sidewalk to driving a minivan down I-35. Our standard isn't student life anymore. It's mom life—the small humans under our wings require care twenty-four hours a day. So when we slack off, it matters, even if our slacking off seems small compared to the way we used to be able to sleep for eight consecutive hours, or stop for coffee, or hang out with friends.

I don't mean that we should fixate every waking moment on our children and disregard all else. I'm talking about true selfishness: the choice to ignore the fight in the playroom in favor of five or ten or a hundred more minutes of social media or phone time or a book or Netflix binge. It's the choice to treat our children like a group or a herd rather than as individuals with unique needs for a one-on-one relationship with us. It's the choice to see their chores and contributions as something we're entitled to have them do—to make it about us instead of their well-being and growth.

Shame, Guilt, and the Gospel

Yes, bad mothering is real, and I've barely scratched the surface of all the forms it can take. But it is one of those things that creates so much shame and guilt in women that it is rarely talked about except humorously or as a means for gaining pity from others. Moms confess their badness to other moms, but only to receive sympathy, not to change. (Ask me how I know—I'm guilty!)

Why so much shame? Why are mothers the most guilt-ridden creatures on the planet? I'm not completely sure, but I think the pressure of daily sustaining tiny people's lives may have something to do with it. The acknowledgment that we're messing up seems the worst thing we could say about ourselves in light of the weightiness of our soul-shaping, life-preserving occupation. We know that our actions or inactions could set a course for another human that is marked by pain or sorrow or self-loathing or failure, and what if it lasts longer than a lifetime and into eternal torment?

So we tend toward these false choices: either acknowledge the serious nature of our job and be crushed under the weight of it or shrug it off as no big deal so our failures don't really matter. At this point, Christian moms are used to hearing, "You can't ruin your children! God can save them despite you!" And that is true, and I am so glad that God can and does see fit to save the most unlikely of sons and daughters. I am so grateful that he did it for me and that none of us or our children are beyond his reach.

But rather than soothing our fears by minimizing our God-given calling to be good mothers who bring up our kids in the Lord, we can truly be free of fear, guilt, and perfectionism only at the foot of the cross. It's at the cross that we lay down our indifference and our fears about the work set before us in shepherding eternal souls in favor of full investment and commitment to the job. And it's at the cross that we share the yoke of the burden that work creates with the strongest person in the universe so that we are not crushed under its weight.

When we mothers soak our children's existence with the lived-out goodness that says, "My life for yours," we work the gospel into them from top to toe. It is a force stronger than we dare imagine. And when we don't do it, it matters. Can God save your children despite you? Of course. But if you're a Christian mother, he means to do it with you as an integral part of the story. Does being a sacrificial Christian mother ensure your child's salvation? By no means. But rest assured that if he saves your children, he intends to use you as one of the pointers to his glorious, saving face.

Christ's goodness transforms *our* hearts and actions to good. It is not because we're better or we've earned it, not because we're no longer sinful. We aren't the Savior; we're his ambassadors. We know the goodness of another. We can be good mothers because we've tasted and seen that the Lord is good, and now we give tastes of him to our children as the goodness pours out of us. We can be good mothers because Christ laid down his life for us; therefore, we can lay down our lives for them. We can be good mothers because we have been forgiven our sins and can forgive our children their sins. We can be good mothers because at the foot of the cross, we can get the grace to repent and turn from every sinful thing we do and be filled with his Spirit. And the fruit of that Spirit is goodness.

We can be good mothers only and always because of Christ.

Developing Our Second Bests

G. K. Chesterton says in his "Emancipation of Domesticity" that a woman who has made the home her domain "may develop all her second bests."[20] In a world that runs on specialization, this is an enigma, to be sure.

What do you say to a woman who has made her home and family her priority, aside from, "I could never do that!" A mother's duties are necessarily broad and, therefore, prohibit the kind of narrowness of some professional work. Moms have a variety of interests and abilities, just like everyone else. I love to write, study the Bible, bake, garden, and, every once in a while, get caught up in a knitting project, but I'm far from expert in any of them. The time I devote to these interests is in the nooks and crannies of life: naptime, after bedtime, here and there. A mother's primary time is spent mothering, teaching, preparing meals, cleaning, instructing, laundering, diapering, snuggling, shopping, straightening, and loving.

Chesterton says that "there must be in every center of humanity one human being upon a larger plan; one who does not 'give her best,' but gives her all."[21]

When the children are little, it's easy to think that the time to go deep into an area of interest will never come, that we will perpetually be, as Bilbo puts it, "thin, sort of stretched . . . like butter that has been scraped across too much bread."[22] Yet what amazes me about the merging of our gifts and abilities with motherhood is how God strips and equips us in ways we never could have anticipated.

God gives us gifts and abilities; then he gives us children. And perhaps it seems he's made an error when our gifts and abilities seem completely irrelevant to the job of bringing up children and caring for a home. We may have gotten an A in art history or creative writing or biology, but how does that help us when the laundry pile is at epic levels? We may be used to the feeling of proficiency in our premothering days, having graduated with honors or gotten recommendations from professors or employers, yet how does this transfer into preparing meals with a crying baby on one hip and a toddler who has a natural talent for proving Newton's laws of motion again and again?

Yet your abilities, your education, your hard-earned A's in whatever subject, do have a place in the home. The way you applied yourself then will be needed now. The discipline of study in the classroom has simply reached its goal: real life. And in real life the lessons will be ones that require your all rather than your best. The lessons we must engage in now are of the pass/fail variety. Was there dinner? Yes? Pass. Are there clothes to wear? Yes? Pass. And perhaps the one that undergirds them all: Did you give of yourself all that Christ has given you?

Motherhood Mimics the Cross

In the intense years of mothering, God is molding us, bending us, and stretching us, and even halfway through, we won't be who we were at the beginning. And that's a feature God has put in motherhood, not a bug. If we're the same at the end as we were at the beginning, something has run amok. God is in the business of transforming us, and motherhood is an expedient way to raze and rebuild us.

God will use our history, our past education, and our premotherhood achievements for a purpose we may not immediately like: to show us who we are when they are taken from us. Who are we when we're struggling to nurse a newborn baby who won't latch properly? Who are we when we're thrown into a world of medical supplies and therapy appointments, having discovered that our baby's brain didn't develop normally? In that sense, motherhood mimics the cross; it is the great leveler of women. Babies don't care if you have your doctorate. A child in a tantrum isn't deterred by your 4.0 GPA. This isn't to say that those achievements aren't valuable, but their worth only transfers if they bear fruit in disciplining our character toward greater godliness, greater Christlikeness.

So, mothers, be liberated from the need to chase after being the best and, instead, give your all to all that God has put before you. Give your all in story telling, give your all to making dirty things clean again, give your all to the meals that must get into the tummies, give your all to training your people in righteousness, and give your all in the nooks and crannies of life to your unique interests.

When we look at Christ's work for us, we see that he held nothing back. If what Paul says in Colossians is true—that Christ made *all things*, that he is before *all things*, that he holds *all things* together, and that *all things* are being reconciled to God through Christ—then I think it's safe to say that *all things* a Christian mother does have eternal significance. There was nothing half-hearted about Jesus's dying on the cross. As the old hymn reminds us, "Jesus paid it *all*, *all* to him I owe."[23] As mothers we give our all, because that's what Jesus did. We can give our all in the strength and power he supplies.

When we give our all in the ways that seem small but costly, we can't anticipate our future. You never know where God might take you or how the current state of affairs may be shaping you for future service. Just as Bilbo never foresaw his final journey to the undying lands after the years of being stretched thin, so mothers can never know how God is working for us for the years ahead. Hobbits are surprising little things, after all. And I suppose mothers are too.

Discussion Questions

1. What are some of the messages the world gives us about being a mother? How are those different from what the Bible tells us about being a mother?

2. What makes for a bad mother? How do we become good mothers?

3. How can we give our all in our mothering without making it all about us but all about Christ?

11

Working Women

Whatever you do, work heartily, as for the Lord and not for men, knowing that from the Lord you will receive the inheritance as your reward. You are serving the Lord Christ. *Colossians 3:23–24*

For we are his workmanship, created in Christ Jesus for good works, which God prepared beforehand, that we should walk in them. *Ephesians 2:10*

What has the power to set a woman on edge and make her feel everything from shame to pride to embarrassment to fear? Ask her what she does for a living.

Among Christians, this shouldn't be the case, but, alas, many can attest that it is. Single women may feel that somehow they're missing out on the calling of motherhood and wish they didn't have to work at a job. Others may be happy to forgo husband and kids and find joy in a career. If a mom works outside the home, she may fear judgment, whether real or imagined, from the stay-at-home-mom contingent. If a mom has embraced homemaking full-time, she similarly tends to feel judgment, real or imagined, by her working counterpart. Or, better put, real *and* imagined, for both women.

Before wading into fraught waters, can we take a moment to try to lay aside our presumptions? We might assume that because a woman prioritizes her home such that she has no paycheck, she is ardently opposed to any work outside of it, and we also may assume that because a woman is getting a paycheck, she disdains the work of the home. These are unkind and dangerous presumptions that create inflated divisions in Christ's body.

We also need to recognize our goal as Christian women; it's not the freedom to do whatever we want apart from God but the freedom to do God's will. We want this for ourselves and our fellow sisters in Christ. What principles, then, does the Bible give us regarding women and work?

First, work is not optional. God put men and women in the garden to work. God gave dominion to them both. Throughout the Scriptures, we see very clearly that men and women are similar but not identical. It follows that our work will be similar, with lots of overlap, but not identical. Men and women are to exercise dominion over the earth, to cultivate, to tend. We are to be devoted to good works for the glory of Christ and the spread of the gospel.

God's Word is not silent in regard to the priorities that women in particular should have. We are made as helpers, coworkers (Gen. 2:18), with the home as a priority (Titus 2:5) and as a place of industry, hospitality, and respite (Prov. 31:10–31). Women are to be fearless in the face of frightening things and submissive to their own husbands, to cultivate inward beauty over outward (1 Pet. 3:1–6). We are to be examples of generous patrons, selfless service, and spiritual mothering (Rom. 16:1–13). Women manage difficult circumstances requiring action and prudence, like Abigail, Jael, and Deborah. Women are to exercise the gifts given to them by God's Spirit in the local church (Rom. 12:6–8; 1 Corinthians 12). And under, in, above, and surrounding all of these principles is the understanding that all she does is by, for, and through Christ (Col. 1:16–17).

Meet Real Needs

The pertinent question for women entering the workforce or motherhood or setting up their home or any sphere of work is this: Am I faithfully obeying God as his child by meeting the genuine needs of others, or am I pursuing self-actualization, self-fulfillment, or selfish ambition apart from him?

Our faithfulness first requires a kind of death—death to self and selfish ambition. Yet death leads to life—life where Christ is working his way into and out of everything we do. What exactly that death looks like will vary from person to person, but in every case it will be a gospel act, a spectacle of crucifixion with Christ.

For a single mom who must earn an income, prioritizing Christ and the home may mean doing what it takes to provide for her kids' needs and spending herself at work and then at home at great cost to herself, for the glory of God and for the good of her children.

For a single woman without kids, it may mean considering cross-cultural missions or walking fearlessly into her job, while saving some reserves for the life of the church or investing in her neighborhood or opening her home, whether it's an apartment or a house or a room, so she can share what she has, especially Christ in her.

For a married, stay-at-home mom of littles, it may mean seemingly endless physical tasks and training, laying down the premotherhood feelings of proficiency as she can no longer earn an A for her hard work or receive a promotion.

For the mom with a job that helps financially but isn't essential, it may mean laying that job down and the extra financial cushion so that she can intentionally sow seeds of the gospel in her children. Or it might mean keeping that job and using her gifts to serve others.

For the woman whose husband is facing long-term unemployment or disability, it may mean becoming the breadwinner or caretaker, shouldering a larger portion of responsibility than she had perhaps desired.

For a mom whose children are older and gaining independence, it may mean a shift in the type of work she does, bravely considering the options and doing things she hasn't done in a long time, or trying something brand new.

Faithfully Walking through Your Actual Life

Sometimes our circumstances aren't ideal. *Often* they are not ideal. This isn't heaven. And the call to lay down our lives will take different forms. But this is our calling, with its countless manifestations, but not because we're the one who finally will save our kids or our family or our neighbors or ourselves. We're not Christ. But we are Christians. We gladly follow the God-Man who laid down his own life to meet our truest needs. We gladly echo his great sacrifice in our little deaths to self.

We seek to faithfully live the actual life God has given us, not the one we hoped for or wish we had. We take the principles God himself has given us—for work and dominion, the priority of the home, generosity and hospitality, caring for the children and adults (their bodies and souls)—and we apply them to the real life in front of us. Not the ideal. Not the fantasy. But the actual life God has given us.

The everyday lives of Christian women will not all look the same. Yet our hearts will be united more deeply than any exclusive gathering of women who work or stay at home or work from home or any other category, because of our clinging together to Christ.

Make Much of Jesus

We understand what faithfulness looks like in our specific situation through the guidance God himself gives us in his Word, by his

Spirit, and through the counsel of our local church. Our covenant community and the relationships within it provide the context where we figure out what it means to apply biblical principles to our particular life. The matrix of God's Word, God's Spirit, and God's people is where we go to get wisdom.

Our work—whether in the home or out of it—is not about us. It's not about making a name for ourselves with a fabulous career or being superior because things went well for us and we're doing it all "right" or trying to "have it all." If we ache to make a name for ourselves, in self-glorification, we should remember that we serve the One whose name is above all names. He will not suffer us as competitors. And far better than making a name for ourselves, he's written our names in his book, not because we have a great job but because we're his children.

So work really hard. Do amazingly good work. Excel in every single way that you can, in every single area that you can, with the self-forgetful happiness that can be found only when you've laid yourself down and are trusting in the name of a tireless, serving Savior. Trust the author of the Lamb's Book of Life to guide you in every circumstance to every good work that he's prepared for you.

Work Is Ordering

All work is an ordering, reordering, keeping of order, or discovery of order. Or at least all good work should be. A doctor checks the body. He makes sure it's in order. He reorders what's in disorder if possible. A scientist discovers the order of a thing, testing it, trying it, and telling people about it. Then they may turn to utilize that order for further good. Parents order little people. They instruct, discipline, and teach. They bring order and structure to humanity.

A housekeeper orders and reorders a home. A cook orders raw ingredients. A businessperson orders people, ideas, systems, and data. A painter orders liquid color. An accountant properly orders numbers, money, and laws. A writer orders words. A minister of the gospel orders people's hearts.

Right ordering has a satisfaction to it, and the more order and discipline we bring to a thing, the more enjoyment we get out of it. This is one reason that God is perfectly happy. He is perfectly ordered, and all he does is perfectly fulfilled. He couldn't do better or go farther. His works are all brought to full completion, full order.

The more we love his ordering of things, the more we know him as beautifully ordered in himself, the more content we will be with how he's ordered us, our womanliness, our bodies, and the more willing we will be to take up the mantle of work, or ordering, he's put in our life.

One of the difficulties to our ordering of things as women—our external work—is our internal ordering. A disordered mind and heart may be evidenced in both a pigsty and seeming perfection. We could be a hot mess inside, aching and striving for things to be right with God, ignoring all the evidence to the contrary, and the way we quiet the disorder inside is to make everything perfect outside. Or we may be a different kind of hot mess: the kind that has indulged all manner of distractions on social media and long conversations with person after person, going from house to house, all to avoid the real work God has assigned to us. Or, if you're like me, you could even vacillate between the two!

But one thing is clear: a disordered mind and heart aren't free to do good works. Repent and believe the good news and receive the work Christ has done on your behalf. Participate in the ordering he has for your life through submission to him. Look around and see that the design of submission is written everywhere in this world: the earth submits and receives from the sun, the moon, the wind, the weather; a tree submits and receives from the ground the soil, the rain; wood receives a nail; a pillow succumbs to a head laid down on it, as does a horse to a saddle and bridle, an employee to an employer, a child to parents, a woman to her man, the church to Christ, and Christ to God.

We are part of God's work, which means we are ordered. And it means we get to imitate this most divine of activities in a limited way. We don't control things the way God does, and so our efforts will be frustrated by the fall and outside circumstances often enough. But let's not give up. We get to bring order in our varied areas of work as God deems best, and in so doing we must remember, *we are serving the Lord Christ*. Our work matters.

Discussion Questions

1. What does the Bible have to say about whether people should work? What principles does he give us regarding work?

2. What people and circumstances has God put in your life that ought to shape the kind of work you do each day?

3. Are you willing to lay down your preferences and personal longings to do the work God has put before you? Are you willing to "work heartily as to the Lord" in the areas you enjoy and the areas you find challenging?

12

Discipling Women

Him we proclaim, warning everyone and teaching everyone with all wisdom, that we may present everyone mature in Christ. *Colossians 1:28*

For though you have countless guides in Christ, you do not have many fathers. For I became your father in Christ Jesus through the gospel. *1 Corinthians 4:15*

I still remember the tagline of the evangelism and discipleship program that my youth group used during my middle school and high school years: "Build. Equip. Win." We were taught how to build people up in their knowledge of God, how to equip them with the Word, and then how to win them as disciples of Jesus. What I didn't realize was that *I* was actually being discipled by my pastor and the adult volunteers through that program, even as I thought I was just there to help those who *really* needed it. In learning how to come alongside others, *I* was taught what it meant to follow Jesus. *I* got a front seat to the faithfulness of the volunteer ministers in youth group; *I* was taught God's Word; *I* was up to my eyeballs in Bible studies and prayer groups. Even as I reached out to friends and strangers, trying to reach them with God's love, it was my heart that was being caught up in the glory of Christ and being captured by his beauty.

Discipleship is the most flexible, scrappy, succulent-like thing I've ever encountered. It can flourish with the tiniest seed and the sparest water. What do I mean by that? I mean that it's irrepressible. If you're a woman with no older Christian women around you to disciple you, somehow God will make sure you grow up in him. Maybe he'll do it directly through his Spirit and his Word. Maybe he'll use a woman long dead who wrote a book a hundred years ago in a different country than you live in to grow you up in him. Maybe he'll use godly women whom you barely know but have opportunity to observe from a distance. He could use texts or emails or the writing of brothers and sisters on the Internet to disciple you, or Facebook, of all the crazy things.

Discipleship is irrepressible and unstoppable because our God is irrepressible and unstoppable in the lives of his children. He will not leave you alone. Paul puts it this way:

> What then is Apollos? What is Paul? Servants through whom you believed, as the Lord assigned to each. I planted, Apollos watered, but God gave the growth. So neither he who plants nor he who waters is anything, but only God who gives the growth. (1 Cor. 3:5–7)

When we realize that God is the growth giver, we recognize that he can use his people in surprisingly unconventional ways to disciple those he's calling to himself. This should give us huge confidence as we seek to grow and to make disciples. If God is the main mover, we can trust that he will accomplish his purpose to save and mature his people.

The Goal of Discipling

What is disciple making? David Mathis calls it "spiritual parenting."[24] He says, "It is personal attention and guidance from one spiritual generation to the next."[25] If there's no similarity between motherhood and discipleship, we're doing it wrong. Titus 2 describes this woman-to-woman disciple making like this:

> Older women likewise are to be reverent in behavior, not slanderers or slaves to much wine. They are to teach what is good, and so train the young women to love their husbands and children, to be self-controlled, pure, working at home, kind, and submissive to their own husbands, that the word of God may not be reviled." (vv. 3–6)

When it comes to having children, spiritual ones are the only kind that last. A biological mother is as barren as a twig if her children are not her spiritual children. And a barren woman may be as fertile as the Nile with her spiritual sons and daughters.

Back when my oldest kids were babies, I attempted a number of knitting projects. My grandmother was a wonderful knitter and crocheter. She had taught me a little bit when I was a girl, but she passed away when I was sixteen and wasn't around to help me develop my skills. I bought a knitting book as thick as the Bible and set to deciphering the codes of knitting language. It was pretty rough, and in the end I was stuck with choosing only the simplest of patterns because I didn't have a teacher who could show me over and over in person how to do the stitches. I ended up completing some simple items that were hard won. Titus 2 shows us a different picture.

A Titus 2 disciple has an older woman there to tell her to take a deep breath when she feels offended by a passage of Scripture. She has someone sitting with her through the tension and skillfully handling God's Word before her eyes; in other words, she has a master knitter on hand to patiently show her the stitches of life in Christ. This older woman is passing on easy recipes to feed a crowd so that hospitality can start to grow, and giving suggestions for schedules and organization in the hopes that a well-managed home will be freed up for the work of the ministry. She has a keen eye for spotting all the ways God is already at work in this younger disciple and points them out. And she's doing all these things tailor made for the woman in front of her—shoring up *her* weaknesses, giving thanks for *her* strengths, and in all things holding out Christ and his Word.

Teaching to Learn, Learning to Teach

Sometimes the way God grows us up is by forcing us to teach others. Maybe we're longing for that ideal older woman of Titus 2 to shower her wisdom down on us. But perhaps God wants to use that longing as the catalyst that drives us to become the older, wiser, woman we wish we had. We never learn quite so well as when we teach.

In the end, our goal is simply this: to make Christ the center and goal of every relationship to the glory of God. Dietrich Bonhoeffer says:

> The call of Jesus teaches us that our relation to the world has been built on an illusion. All the time we thought we had enjoyed a direct relation with men and things. This is what had hindered us from faith and obedience. Now we learn that in the most intimate relationships of life, in our kinship with father and mother, bothers and sisters, in married love, and in our duty to the community, direct relationships are impossible. Since the coming of Christ, his followers have no more immediate realities of their own, not in their family relationships nor in the ties with their nation nor in the relationships formed in the process of living. Between father and son, husband and wife, the individual and the nation, stands Christ the Mediator,

whether they are able to recognize him or not. We cannot establish direct contact outside ourselves except through him, through his word, and through our following of him. To think otherwise is to deceive ourselves.[26]

Bringing Christ into every interaction and every relationship is the work of disciple making—not because we actually need to bring him there, as if he wasn't there already, but because we become dulled to his presence. We think we can see things rightly and grow without him. We act as though our relationships and interactions happen irrespective of him, when in fact *nothing* happens irrespective of him. Disciple making is helping others to see Christ for what he is: before all things, holding all things together, all in all. And in helping others, our own faith is made sight.

Discussion Questions

1. Are there women in your life who have raised you up in the Lord, teaching you to be a disciple of Jesus? Who? If not, how have you grown in the Lord?

2. How can you continue to learn from other Christians in order to be brought to maturity in Christ?

3. Who can you begin to nurture in the Lord, teaching them about Jesus and helping them better understand how to apply God's Word to their lives?

PART 3

FEARLESS AND FREE WOMEN—IN CHRIST

To him be glory in the church and in Christ Jesus throughout all generations, forever and ever. Amen.
Ephesians 3:21

13

Strong and Weak Women

He said to me, "My grace is sufficient for you, for my power is made perfect in weakness." Therefore I will boast all the more gladly of my weaknesses, so that the power of Christ may rest upon me. *2 Corinthians 12:9*

Who is this who looks down like the dawn,
   beautiful as the moon, bright as the sun,
   awesome as an army with banners?" (Song 6:10)

Who indeed? A woman, of course.

Where but in the Scriptures could we find womanhood as glorious as this? Who but our God could design something with such blinding beauty alongside robust strength? Psalms and Proverbs fill out this vision of a woman who shows us fortitude clothed in splendor—a woman who presides over her domain with strong arms and resourcefulness (Prov. 31:10–31); daughters that are corner pillars, whose strong support could only be matched by their exquisiteness (Ps. 144:12).

Strength such as this seems hard to disagree with, even for the world. Who wouldn't admire this kind of strength and beauty? Yet, regrettably, the world urges us to exchange this sort of strength for a competition obsessed with measuring sticks. It seems in our culture a woman is strong only if she is so *compared to a man*. Rather than finding relevance in the uniqueness of womanly strength, we belittle and degrade it, finding meaning and value only in impossible apples-to-oranges comparisons. It is a sad consolation that trades the glory of feminine strength for a treadmill race to nowhere.

Sometimes Christian women who would recoil from competition with men engage in another sort, one with other women. As long as they can come out ahead of the woman next to them, all's well. We say we want equality, but that's usually true only when we've got the short end of the stick.

The Glory of Inequality

Elisabeth Elliot said, "Our inequalities are . . . essential to the image of God."[27] This was her provocative way of saying that men and women are different—she wasn't saying that their worth or value is unequal. She simply means that we are different and given different but overlapping roles. For male and female, there exists a certain sort of equality in the inequality, meaning that the inequality goes both ways. I've yet to meet a man who could grow a human in his body and birth it into the world, even as some women who've tried to make themselves men claim that they have. And I've never met a woman who could impregnate another, carrying in herself the very seed of life, even as some men who've tried to make themselves women may claim to do.

When we're weak, it's natural to start to envy the strong. Especially our sisters who are so similar to us but just a little better at everything, a little stronger, a little more put together. Joe Rigney says that envy tends to breed closest to home.[28] I spend zero time fretting about the strengths and talents of the Pioneer Woman, Ree

Drummond. I've yet to measure myself up against my heroes in the faith such as Corrie Ten Boom. But how quickly do I take stock of my weaknesses in light of the strengths of my dear friend Christy, whom God has gifted with wonderful organization and hospitality and humor? How fast can I measure my lack next to my big-hearted sister Jessica's fortitude in a foreign country and her sacrifice?

When we see the strength of our sisters in Christ and see our own weakness, there doesn't seem to be any sort of equality in the inequality. And lest we try to force that sort of equality, we should hear this from our Lord through Paul:

> For by the grace given to me I say to everyone among you not to think of himself more highly than he ought to think, but to think with sober judgment, each according to the measure of faith that God has assigned. For as in one body we have many members, and the members do not all have the same function, so we, though many, are one body in Christ, and individually members one of another. Having gifts that differ according to the grace given to us, let us use them: if prophecy, in proportion to our faith; if service, in our serving; the one who teaches, in his teaching; the one who exhorts, in his exhortation; the one who contributes, in generosity; the one who leads, with zeal; the one who does acts of mercy, with cheerfulness. (Rom. 12:3–8)

What Is the Real Thief of Joy?

There is no equality in God's gifts. He is free to give as he chooses—that's the nature of a gift. We are not owed equality, no matter what lies our American ethic has tried to sew into the fabric of our minds. We must grab our seam rippers and tear those lies out. The simple fact that some have been gifted with more than others doesn't lessen the value he's bestowed on each.

The other remarkable thing about the passage above is that God expects us to measure our faith in light of others'. He expects that we'll notice discrepancies, and this is supposed to make us humble and sober, not whiny and entitled. There is an alternative to being depressed by comparison. There is an alternative to letting it steal our joy—it's that we would be humbled by it and that we would get serious about serving the Lord with the portion he's given us. What if the thief of joy isn't comparison, as Theodore Roosevelt said, but our unwillingness to rejoice in the gifts of others? What if keeping our heads down so that we won't accidentally notice how great someone else is doing and be envious is really just the evidence of a shriveled heart, unable to be thankful to God for others' successes? I know women intent on fertilizing a thousand acres with the small hill of manure they've been given, constantly learning and gleaning from those around them, unafraid of how they might measure up. Others sit atop their vast pile of gifts and make mud pies. Oh, that we would let the measure of our faith—whether small or large—fuel the fire in us to use our gifts for God.

But what do we do when our weaknesses seem stronger than our strengths? What happens when the measure of our faith is minuscule and our giftings swallowed by our frailty? That's when we do something very strange: we brag. As we hold tight to Jesus, whom our minuscule faith is wholly set on, we own our weakness and boast in it.

> He said to me, "My grace is sufficient for you, for my power is made perfect in weakness." Therefore I will boast all the more gladly of my weaknesses, so that the power of Christ may rest upon me. For the sake of Christ, then, I am content with weaknesses, insults, hardships, persecutions, and calamities. For when I am weak, then I am strong. (2 Cor. 12:9–10)

Deprived, Yet Full

Sleep deprivation is a big part of my life as a mom with a special-needs son who has neurological sleep problems. Our son is four, and he's the youngest of five children, so I've spent a fair amount of life underslept, but never so bad as the last four years. You can imagine how weak I've felt these past years. Even more than that, I've been desperate, crazy, at the end of my rope, under siege, and everything opposite of strong—not to mention ridiculously, deliriously tired.

If someone would have told me four years ago that I'd be facing years of significant sleep deprivation with no end in sight, I would have said, "I can't do that. Wrong person. Without enough sleep I become irrational, depressed, forgetful, and a little crazy."

So how is it that I'm sitting here typing away rather than being a puddle on the floor? How is that when I *am* a puddle on the floor (which is often enough!), there's somehow grace enough in the paper towel roll? How is there laughter and silliness at home? How are there relationships of fruitfulness and gospel growth? In other words, how is there a life that is robust and seemingly led by a strong woman, which I know deep in my bones I am not?

He did it the way he always does—by confounding the wisdom of the world, by shocking me with his grace. By lifting the head of a lowly mom who gets little sleep caring for her special son and making all grace abound during the days of strength and faith and giftedness and the days of being a puddle. He also did it through my strong sisters and brothers in Christ.

When we're weak, we need the strength of the strong. We need their sacrifice of service when they bring meals and grocery shop for us. We need their faith poured out for us in prayer. We need their exhortations and admonishments. We need their generosity, their mercy, their leadership. How does God make us strong when we're weak? He does it through Christ. And he does it through Christ's body—in its glorious inequality.

I don't know if you feel strong or weak. I don't know if you feel competent for the life you've been given, with a clear understanding of your measure of faith, abilities, and gifts. But I know he's given you something, whether small or large or middling. Don't scoff at it, because its measure is different from the sister or brother next to you.

I also know that if you feel that you have no strength, nothing to offer, no ability in yourself, you may be in the most powerful position of all, the one where he comes down and is your strength in weakness and frailty. The one where your boast is not in your gifts but in your shortcoming and your decrease—and Christ in that shortcoming, Christ's increase in your decrease. May he bless you with his apportioned measure of faith and gifts, and in the times of leanness, may he bless you all the more with himself.

Discussion Questions

1. Do you recoil at the truth that we are not given an equal measure of gifts or faith by the Lord?

2. Do you tend to look at other people's circumstances or gifts with an edge of envy? What would it look like for you to be free of envy and instead delight in others, with the heart of a learner and sister in the Lord?

3. How can you begin boasting in the Lord when he puts you in circumstances that make you weak? How would that change your view of hardship and weakness?

14

Dependent Women

My God will supply every need of yours according to his riches in glory in Christ Jesus. *Philippians 4:19*

But now in Christ Jesus you who once were far off have been brought near by the blood of Christ. *Ephesians 2:13*

Parents need to be willing to yell at their kids. That's probably not what you're used to hearing, because most of the yelling that we parents do at our kids is sinful and pretty ugly. But every now and then, there's a situation that requires a yell because of the extreme urgency and danger at hand. It's not that we're yelling *at* them exactly, but more like we're yelling *for* them, for their good and safety.

A few years ago, our youngest son was in a tough place development-wise, which is to say, not a lot of developing was happening. During the first year of his life, our doctors thought it was probable that he had a degenerative brain condition. That's just code for "he may not live very long." So every neurology appointment we went to (and there were more than I wish to recount) I was asked, "Any signs of deterioration? Have you noticed a plateau?" It didn't matter how positive I felt going into the appointment; those questions would flatten me because sometimes I just didn't know what my answer was. Sometimes his progress was almost imperceptible, and I wondered if I was just conjuring up his "progress" out of a mom's wishful thinking.

Praying with My Hand over My Mouth

During that time, my prayers were veering into despondency, and my heart was consumed with fear. And as timing would have it, my Bible reading plan had me in Job. Sometimes God is subtle; sometimes not so much. Here I was faced with the actualization of my worst fear. Job had lost all his children. That fear made me feel like I was on the Dawn Treader in Narnia in the Lone Islands approaching the terrifying darkness, "the Island where Dreams come true," only Edmund and Lucy discover it's not what they think. Instead of dreams coming true, it's nightmares.[29]

Apart from seeing my worst fear actualized in Job, I also was confronted by a yelling God. In Job 38–42 God tells us some big things about himself. We always say we want God to answer our prayers, that we want to hear from him, but I wonder if the answers he gives in Job are quite what we have in mind. We know that God is big enough to handle our fears, our questions, and our hearts, but can we handle his answers to those fears and questions?

We may think that because we're desperate and scared, God owes us a warm, gooey brownie-hug of relief. But our desperation is meant to lead us to dependence, and dependence doesn't often come through having our desperation relieved or slathered in chocolate.

When we are scared about our future or about our present or about our past, sometimes God loves us with the shout of a Father who yells for his children as they are about to step out into the street unaware. He grabs our arm and snatches us away from danger and terrifies us with his love. God keeps us from what would really harm us—a mistrustful, wayward heart—even as he allows the cause of our earthly desperation to remain.

> Then Job answered the LORD and said:
>
> > "Behold, I am of small account; what shall I answer you?
> > > I lay my hand on my mouth.
> > I have spoken once, and I will not answer;
> > > twice, but I will proceed no further." (Job 40:3–5)

This text is not oft quoted in messages about the importance and power of prayer. Yet, here Job reminds us that there is time for dependence and trust and a quieting of our complaint before God, even as we know from the Psalms that we have grounds to air our complaint as well. We can prayerfully commune in dependence on the Lord with our hand over our mouth.

All Our Needs

How do we learn contentment and prayerful dependence when God seems to be withholding good things from us? We desire our children to be saved, faithful marriages, good and meaningful jobs with financial security and the ability to give generously, and close community in Christ. How could God be opposed to these things that, from our view, would so clearly bring him glory?

Like Job, we are baffled by what's happening in our life. But in Christ, God has answered us decisively. In Christ we have irrefutable proof that God is for us. Look at him there on the cross, see his empty tomb, and, like Job, lay your hand over your mouth as God terrifies you with the lengths he goes to show his love.

How does God supply every need of ours? By meeting every need with Christ. In order to wrap our minds around this, we have to start sorting out what our real needs are. What do we need? We need God's wrath removed from us. We need someone to crush the

Serpent's head with his heel. We need our sins forgiven. We need to be made alive. We need a new heart. We need the gift of faith. We need to be made holy. We need resurrection. We need an imperishable body. We need a way for fellowship and communion with God our Father. We need someone to send a Comforter, Counselor, and Helper to walk with us *now*. Oh, our needs are so many and so great! In Christ, God has met every one of them.

Our son didn't die. He's sitting next to me in my chair right now, resting his sleeping head on my arm. While I type, the movement of my arm makes his little face bobble. But someday he will die. So will the rest of my children and my husband and me and every person I love. So we must get this settled, dear sisters. There is only one hope in this life strong enough to keep you, and it's the resurrection hope. It's the hope of the life to come, the hope that even when we die, our lives cannot be touched or harmed because they are hidden in Christ forever and that God himself is our reward.

God does not despise our desperation. It's his way of drawing us near, helping us become dependent and keeping us from ruining our lives. So go to Jesus. It's never the wrong time. All our reasons for staying away are the very reasons we need him. "All the fitness He requireth, is to feel your need of him":

Come ye sinners, poor and needy,
Weak and wounded, sick and sore;
Jesus ready stands to save you,
Full of pity, love, and pow'r.

Come, ye thirsty, come and welcome,
God's free bounty glorify;
True belief and true repentance,
Ev'ry grace that brings you nigh.

Come ye weary, heavy laden,
Lost and ruined by the fall;

If you tarry till you're better,
You will never come at all.

Let not conscience make you linger,
Nor of fitness fondly dream;
All the fitness He requireth
Is to feel your need of Him.

I will arise and go to Jesus,
He will embrace me in His arms;
In the arms of my dear Savior,
O there are ten thousand charms.[30]

Discussion Questions

1. Have you ever been in a desperate situation that made you sense how powerless you are? What was that like?

2. Did this desperate situation alienate you from God or draw you closer to him?

3. How can you begin to pray and trust that God will use every desperate situation he puts you in to make you dependent on him for your good?

15

Afflicted Women

I am sure that neither death nor life, nor angels nor rulers, nor things present nor things to come, nor powers, nor height nor depth, nor anything else in all creation, will be able to separate us from the love of God in Christ Jesus our Lord. *Romans 8:38–39*

When God gives me hard things or takes things away from me that I want to keep, usually my first response is to think he's bankrupting me. We all have this tendency to think that God is shrinking us when he's really growing us. We think that when he's pruning, when he's causing pain, that the purpose is really just to make us small and to do us harm. We think that our decreasing is the end of the story. We forget that in our decreasing, he is increasing. We believe that our affliction is a net loss for us, when really it is the most gigantic gain imaginable.

We're single, and the singleness feels like deprivation. We're married, and the married life is nothing like what we expected. We're moms, and being a mom feels like a thousand deaths to our preferences and sanity. We're working, and our jobs feel like they're unimportant or ridiculous or impossible, like we've been given a stone, not bread. We're waiting to be grandmothers, and it feels like the crown of growing old has been denied to us.

And I haven't even hit on major suffering yet: the child who dies, the spouse who leaves, the parent who abuses and hates or neglects and ignores, chronic illness, lifelong disability, unrelenting infertility, much-loved wayward family who mistrust God and you. Then we can move from our personal suffering to the suffering running rampant in the world: disease, starvation, orphans, wars, women in bondage to men, pornography sweeping the globe via the Internet, sex trafficking.

Deep down, if we think that there's nothing behind it, that we're just left pruned to the point of no return, we really will wither on the vine. We must know all through the marrow of our bones that after death comes life. The life God's given us, with all its trials and sufferings, is working growth and expansion for us in an unseen realm. We're getting taller, growing thicker, and becoming established in him.

We may think that by giving up our bodies to babies, giving up our free time to supper prep and laundry, giving up our night out with friends for going over the finances, or by giving up the desire to have all those things, we're being squelched. But we're being shaped. We're being grown out of death and into a likeness. God can do it through making us single, married, infertile, disabled, divorced, mothers, grandmothers, godmothers, and anything else he plans.

Spare Us Those Blessings

If we're honest with ourselves, most of us would have to admit that while we ask for God's blessings, we don't really want them. Not on his terms anyway. If a blessing means wealth or ease or having our expectations met, we're all in, but when it means dependence and pain, we quickly ask the Lord to spare us those blessings.

Isn't this what consumes so many of our prayers and thoughts, what fills our anxious minds at night: the fear that the Lord might bless us with suffering? We can do without those blessings, we think. Jesus's ideas about blessing don't match up with ours.

And he opened his mouth and taught them, saying:
Blessed are the poor in spirit, for theirs is the kingdom of heaven.
Blessed are those who mourn, for they shall be comforted.
Blessed are the meek, for they shall inherit the earth.
Blessed are those who hunger and thirst for righteousness, for they shall be satisfied.
Blessed are the merciful, for they shall receive mercy.
Blessed are the pure in heart, for they shall see God.
Blessed are the peacemakers, for they shall be called sons of God.
Blessed are those who are persecuted for righteousness' sake, for theirs is the kingdom of heaven.
Blessed are you when others revile you and persecute you and utter all kinds of evil against you falsely on my account. (Matt. 5:2–11)

Vaneetha Risner, who contracted polio at a young age and has endured every manner of suffering since, including the loss of a child, divorce, and debilitating post-polio syndrome, speaks poignantly about our misconceptions of blessing. Quoting a study Bible, she says, "The Greek word translated 'blessed' in these passages is *makarioi,* which means to be fully satisfied. It refers to those receiving God's favor, *regardless of the circumstances.*"[31] Vaneetha asks:

What is blessing, then? Scripture shows that blessing is anything God gives that makes us fully satisfied in him. Anything that draws us closer to Jesus. Anything that helps us relinquish the temporal and hold on more tightly to the eternal. And often it is the struggles and trials, the aching disappointments and the unfulfilled longings that best enable us to do that.[32]

Martin Luther had his pulse on this reality when he prescribed three steps for studying the Bible: prayer, meditation, and *trials*.[33] Never do I drink as deeply of the living water of the Word as when I've been thrown down a well and drenched with Christ's presence. How easy it is to confuse being drenched with being drowned. Never is the Bible as potent as when trials have swallowed me up and communion with Christ is found in the rotting belly of a fish.

How do we become mature in Christ? Maturity is a path through suffering with Christ. As much as we wish to spare ourselves and our loved ones pain, dear sisters, we dare not rob them of God's blessing, that is, the realization that he is the true light "when all other lights go out."[34] God's blessing is himself. Suffering is the terms of discovering *our* dependence and need and the *abundance* of Christ's presence. Affliction is the way we learn that nothing can separate us from his love. In Christ, love is the theme, the heartbeat, the melody, and the storyline of suffering. Affliction makes this love song sing out all the louder as the noise and pain of the world try in vain to muffle it.

The Fellowship of Suffering

When we realized our son had some significant disabilities, I had the strange thought, *Does this mean we have to get all new friends?* I could feel the ground shifting beneath me, and I hadn't figured out whether this was a *defining* reality. I didn't know whether people outside of our experience of disability would be able to sufficiently relate to us and the suffering we were undergoing in order to maintain meaningful relationships. The truth is, some couldn't, but most could. It was an odd question for a *Christian* to seriously consider, because in the body of Christ, the highest and most meaningful realm of connection is not with those who are like us based on external circumstances but with those who are very much *not* like us externally but have been adopted into the same family, with shared life in Christ. So even if we were the only people in our whole acquaintance with a disabled child, we need not fear that we will go without the most necessary human, Christian connections.

The shared-suffering interest groups that form in Christian settings are often helpful and do just what a gathering of Christians ought to do: "Admonish the idle, encourage the fainthearted, help the weak, be patient with them" (1 Thess. 5:14). They provide a place where we can walk with other Christians facing similar circumstances who may be able to guide us more skillfully than someone who hasn't faced what we're going through. But there are other places where I see women especially, more and more *isolated* to their particular group. Sometimes it's a group for young moms, adoptive parents, married women, women struggling with infertility, special-needs parents, single women, divorced women, abuse victims, or some other group.

While these types of groups can be very helpful, staying in groups such as these *singularly* and for a prolonged time may multiply our blind spots. We lack the input of people whose experience is different from ours, which is essential to growth and development. Shared experience is a powerful comfort, but it is not the deepest comfort. Our God knows that the inherent sinfulness in all of us distorts even our areas of suffering into opportunities for sin.

When we surround ourselves exclusively with those who also have experienced similar hardships, the temptation to paint a narrative of good and evil, with ourselves as the heroine and everyone who hasn't experienced what we have as the villain, can be irresistible.

We need people who aren't in our exact place of difficulty to say things that occasionally rub us the wrong way. We need to give people permission to be truthful in their words to us without making them fear every word will be pulled apart and examined for tone perfection. We need to hear things that give us a different perspective and acknowledge that the person saying them loves us. Sometimes we must help correct people who are out to lunch, who are like Job's friends, or we have to set boundaries with people who needlessly hurt us. But often enough, we just need to let our Christian friends be our Christian friends—different from us but in the same family, loving us, however imperfectly.

Our own suffering changes the way we interact with others in their suffering. Rather than trying to solve their problem of suffering, we start coming alongside them to help them live through it as Christians. Rather than try to fix them or their circumstances, we become keenly aware that control of those things is beyond us and instead we are free to love. So even as we bear with the sometimes unhelpful remarks of others, we can use our own times of affliction to teach us a better way to be there for others.

The fellowship of suffering is only an actual fellowship insomuch as the common bond is the bond of Christ. In other words, what makes my suffering an occasion for fellowship isn't that the other people have experienced the *exact same thing* I have; it's that *in Christ* my suffering is shared with them through Christ, and their suffering is shared with me through Christ. "If one member suffers, all suffer together; if one member is honored, all rejoice together" (1 Cor. 12:26).

Every Circumstance Bows to His Love for Us

When our youngest son was just six months old, he wasn't lifting his head up and had very low muscle tone. I was used to holding him with his head always resting on my shoulder or chest and his cozy body piled on me. It felt quite normal. A dear friend had a son a few months younger than our Titus. We had enjoyed pregnancy together and the anticipation of sons. My friend came to our home for a Super Bowl party bursting in the door with arms full of food and bags. Without a thought, I swooped her beautiful baby boy into my arms to relieve her load and found myself quickly discombobulated with such strong feelings of sadness and joy. Here was her son: strong, robust, making eye contact, lifting up his head and able to connect with me the way most babies his age would—but in a way that my son couldn't. I hadn't held any other babies but Titus since Titus was born, and even though my head knew the realities of the difference, feeling them in my arms was another thing.

This could have been an occasion for alienation, but instead it was one for shared suffering and joy. This baby boy of hers was a joy—his health, his strength, his mind. He was a true delight. So was mine. And yet there was sorrow over the loss of a fully able body and brain. It was a sorrow this fellow mom had cried over with me and prayed about with me and had brought meals to lessen our burden. She shared in our affliction, and we shared in her joy, because we were part of the same body in Christ. My former pastor says this of suffering:

Not only is all your affliction momentary, not only is all your affliction light in comparison to eternity and the glory there. But all of it is totally meaningful. Every millisecond of your pain, from the fallen nature or fallen man, every millisecond of your misery in the path of obedience is producing a peculiar glory you will get because of that. I don't care if it was cancer or criticism. I don't care if it was slander or sickness. It wasn't meaningless. It's doing something! It's not meaningless. Of course you can't see what it's doing. Don't look to what is seen. When your mom dies, when your kid dies, when you've got cancer at 40, when a car careens into the sidewalk and takes her out, don't say, "That's meaningless!" It's not. It's working for you an eternal weight of glory.[35]

Yes, it is working glory, and it's also working in us deeper unity and fellowship with Christ himself, even now. Oh, Christian sisters, that we would let our suffering take us deeper into the heart of God in Christ. That we would know how high and how wide and how deep his love is for us—a love that we can never be separated from—because when God gave his Son to us as a sacrifice for sin and then put us in the risen Christ, he was showing us the definition of love (1 John 4:10). In Christ, we are cocooned in love, and every single circumstance we walk through is made to serve his love for us. We can never be taken from his strong hand (John 10:28–29).

Discussion Questions

1. What do you think of when you hear the word *blessing*? How is that similar or different from how the Bible uses the word?

2. How might God be using suffering in your life to bless you with more of himself?

3. How can your suffering or the suffering of other Christians be an opportunity for fellowship with one another and with Christ?

16

Free Women

Yet because of false brothers secretly brought in—who slipped in to spy out our freedom that we have in Christ Jesus, so that they might bring us into slavery—to them we did not yield in submission even for a moment, so that the truth of the gospel might be preserved for you. *Galatians 2:4–5*

For the law of the Spirit of life has set you free in Christ Jesus from the law of sin and death. *Romans 8:2*

I am convinced that many of us women have a submission problem—a giant submission problem. But it isn't mainly that we won't submit to our husbands or church leaders or fellow believers; it's that we won't stop submitting to the world. The biggest problem with women and submission is too much of it in the wrong places. We willingly submit to the world's rules.

When I first began immersing myself in Colossians a couple of summers ago, I knew of one passage on submission that tends to cause some angst. It's a text we've already gone over: "Wives, submit to your husbands, as is fitting in the Lord" (Col. 3:18). It's one of a few passages in the Scriptures on wives' submission that tend toward infamy.

Perhaps less well-known to us is the other "submission" passage in the previous chapter of Colossians. It goes like this:

> If with Christ you died to the elemental spirits of the world, why, as if you were still alive in the world, do you submit to regulations— 'Do not handle, Do not taste, Do not touch' (referring to things that all perish as they are used)—according to human precepts and teachings? These have indeed an appearance of wisdom in promoting self-made religion and asceticism and severity to the body, but they are of no value in stopping the indulgence of the flesh. (Col. 2:20–23)

Women are awash in the teaching and dogma of the world, and they are voluntarily placing themselves under its authority. Some don't even know they're doing it.

More Rules than Leviticus

Does any of this sound familiar? We compel ourselves to wear certain styles, even painful shoes, to keep up with what the stores have told us is fashionable. We clean our homes in a particular way with only particular products. We follow every rule and suggestion given to us by the ubiquitous "they" on how to parent our children and keep them safe from every wisp of risk. We apply bizarre treatments to our bodies because someone told us we must get the toxins out. We stress and strain our muscles three times a week minimum because we believe it's the right thing to do, and maybe, just maybe, we'll keep death at bay (or at least have a flat stomach until it comes for us). We're religious about the kind of candle that can burn in our houses, and the smell of essential oils floats through the air whenever we're around, because we're convinced they're the right remedy to use.

Rules, rules, rules. Not God's rules, but rules nevertheless. And, boy, do they wear us out. Who could ever keep up with the always-changing and ever-increasing sets of rules the world is throwing at us? Who could keep up with the self-made religion we ourselves have constructed?

Eat this, don't eat that. "Do not handle, Do not taste, Do not touch" (Col. 2:21). How many children could easily think Leviticus was lighthearted compared to the intricate manuals and weighty rulebooks their mothers lug around, all conveniently located on the bottomless Internet in their pocket. At least the rules in Leviticus were given by a God who seeks our welfare, not by a world bent on our destruction.

Am I saying it's wrong to follow a certain diet? Or work out? Or clean a particular way? Or use certain health remedies? No. Absolutely not. But it *is* wrong to believe that doing any of those things is right. It's wrong to do them because you trust the world (or yourself) more than Christ.

Christ has given us plenty of work to do until he comes again. The last thing we need is to start working on the to-do list the world has assigned to us. We're to "seek the things that are above" (Col. 3:1). That means we're to "put on . . . compassionate hearts, kindness, humility, meekness, and patience" (Col. 3:12), to bear with and forgive one another, and above all, to love (Col. 3:13–14).

Man-made rules make us promises. They give us a command and say, "If you follow this, you will be happy." But none can deliver. None keep their promises. Even when they do deliver on the front end—when the diet does make us slim and improve our digestion, or the correctly buckled carseat does decrease our risks, or the health remedies and vaccines do keep us free from illness—they can't give us lasting happiness. They can't give us peace in place of our deepest fears. Man-made rules cannot cure us of our most serious disease.

At other times, we may use rules as a cloak of comfort. We would rather have one thousand rules to govern every practical piece of our lives than live in the freedom that Christ offers. We'd rather have "Fifteen Rules on Correct Laundry Practices" and "Ten Rules on How to Load the Dishwasher" and "101 Rules on the Food That Must Not Be Eaten." The rules give us a sense of worth, a sense of having done things right, and the feeling of control.

But what if we evaluated on a different scale entirely? What if we acknowledged that scrapping for worth from rule keeping is anti-gospel? What if we started asking ourselves, "Did I fold the clothes with humility? Did I wash the dishes with love? Did I make the supper with patience? Did I go to work with meekness? Did I buckle the child in faith?"

In other words, we should ask ourselves if we're living as Christians. Rather than believing that supper is a success because we avoided all the ingredients on "The Food That Must Not Be Eaten" list, we could view supper as glorifying to God because we served it in a manner worthy of the Lord, which is to say, with love.

And sometimes avoiding certain foods and loving God and others go hand in hand. Often, our exercise routine is a good way to honor the Lord. But Christians must be able to connect all that we do and don't do to the glory of God, whether we eat or drink or fold clothes or buy food at the store. That's when we know God's work in us has borne fruit—when we can do all things, even abstain, as free people who glorify God.

If, because of love for God and a forsaking of sin, you undertake a new diet, then all that's done in faith pleases God. He sees that heart; he sees that pure motive. But if you've decided to engage in a rule-based way of eating because it's the trend, and the world has convinced you it's the right thing to do and that it makes you better, then you've missed the freedom Christ offers you. You've missed the good news, which is that neither food nor clothing, cleaning nor folding, can commend us to God. But Christ can, and he does.

We must start asking ourselves who we're submitting to. The next time you feel under compulsion to do something a certain way as it relates to "things that all perish" (Col. 2:22), ask yourself why. Is it out of fear or faith? On whose authority? Let's resolve to do all things under the authority and freedom of Christ and refuse to submit again to the yoke of slavery. We are Christian women, which means we are marked by our submission and our freedom, both in what we say yes to and what we refuse.

Practicing Our Righteous Freedom as Women

As a child, I was interested in baking one thing and one thing only: chocolate chip cookies. I even perfected a recipe of Mrs. Field's cookies that contained ground oatmeal and Hershey's bars.[36] I took those cookies to the state fair and came home with a blue ribbon. But that was about the extent of my baking prowess.

As a young (overwhelmed) mom with littles, I scoffed at women who baked their own bread and seemed to invest a lot of time in such things. I distinctly remember wanting to say, "You know you can buy that at the store, right?" It almost seemed that all the breadmakers were out there baking bread just to make the rest of us look bad. And this mind-set of mine wasn't limited to bread making. It extended to any number of areas I deemed "non-essential to survival" where I saw other women excelling. Deep down I wanted it to be true that they simply had more time on their hands or an easier life or a need to prove themselves to be better than everyone else. In some cases I was right—women *do* do things for the wrong motives and some women *do* have more time on their hands. But that is beside the point. I was in bondage because I didn't have a category for free women who do good works out of the freedom they have in Christ to enjoy life in Christ with their work.

I imagine I'm not the only woman who has found herself simply unfamiliar with certain biblical categories and unfamiliar with how to practically incorporate them into her life. Things like loving our neighbor and bringing up our children in the Lord and laying down a sinful attitude toward someone close to us and taking our covetous thoughts captive to Christ before they ruin a friendship are all things we must do as Christians, but many of us are flailing around unsure of how to do them. Seeing other people do these things well is a little like watching them bake bread when you've never done it before. It seems mysteriously hard and something that they must have an innate ability to do. Either you can or you can't. And perhaps we just start to deem them nonessential to our survival.

A number of years ago, in a turn of events involving a very enticing picture on Pinterest and a Very Patient Food Blogger who assumed no previous bread-making expertise and wrote as if to a child, I endeavored to make my first loaves of bread.[37] And because my teacher, the Very Patient Food Blogger, was willing to break down every step and explain every term and answer every question that every person asked in the comments, I was able to successfully make two loaves of bread.

The subsequent delight in my family from making those first loaves of bread catapulted me into more and more bread making. Over the years I've grown my skill set and gained the kind of expertise that comes only from experience—from massive flops and mouth-watering success. I've ventured into pastries and croissants and challah and babka and wild yeast.

And the relevant question is: when was I free in regard to baking? Was it before I learned to make bread or after? Before I learned to bake, I was captive to my false thinking about baking and captive to my inability. After I learned how, I was free to make bread *or* buy bread. I now am free to stay home rather than run to the store when we're out of bread. I am free to grab a few loaves in the bread aisle when it's convenient, *and* I am free to delight my children with one of their favorite foods right out of our oven. Also, I am free to continue growing and learning in bread making. The farther I come in it, the more I realize I've barely scratched the surface of all there is to know.

But quite unlike baking bread, forsaking sin and living in Christ really *are* essential to our survival. We aren't just talking about fun but nonessential hobbies, like baking or knitting or gardening. We're talking about something utterly necessary, the freedom to live as a godly Christian woman.

To understand this freedom, we have to get back to the cross. We must remember that the power of sin was broken there when Jesus died. We must remember that our enslavement to sin was abolished, and we are no longer captive. Instead we are free, not just from sin but to be Christ's and to live holy lives full of good works. Good works earn us nothing before God, but don't mistake that most important fact with thinking that godliness is of no gain for us. Godliness, or growing in good works, is great gain (1 Tim. 6:6).

When we walk by faith, we endeavor to take our first steps of righteous freedom, just as I took my first steps in making bread with no way of knowing how I'd do. The first few times are always the hardest and most uncertain. Once we've learned the ropes a bit, got some dough under our fingernails, done it wrong a few times and then made our adjustments, we can make even fairly complicated recipes seem effortless. *Because they've actually become fairly effortless.*

The same is true in our lives as Christian women. The more practiced we are at repentance, at sacrifice, at righteousness, the more it will become normal, like walking across a room rather than like lifting weights. It may make you nervous to hear all this talk of practicing our Christianity, our holiness. But listen to God speak through John:

> And now, little children, abide in him, so that when he appears we may have confidence and not shrink from him in shame

at his coming. If you know that he is righteous, you may be sure that everyone who practices righteousness has been born of him. See what kind of love the Father has given to us, that we should be called children of God; and so we are. (1 John 2:28–3:1)

Mistaking Freedom for Bondage

Practicing righteousness doesn't cause us to be born of God. It is a sign that we've been born of him. And this is the kind of practice that gives us more freedom than we could possibly imagine. When God urges us toward righteousness, he is loving us and setting us free. If righteous living seems like bondage or a killjoy, the problem is very simple: you don't know God well enough. You haven't learned to trust his love. You haven't experienced his superior joys. You haven't suspended your own judgment long enough to see that he's proving you wrong all over the place. Walking with God is like walking with the light on: not only does it keep you from bumping into things, but it allows you the freedom of vision. C. S. Lewis said, "I believe in Christianity as I believe that the sun has risen: not only because I see it, but because by it I see everything else."[38] From Genesis to Revelation, Christ is the light that God is shining throughout the Scriptures, helping us see, know, and enjoy him.

God tells us through Paul, "For God, who said, 'Let light shine out of darkness,' has shone in our hearts to give the light of the knowledge of the glory of God in the face of Jesus Christ" (2 Cor. 4:6).

The light of Christ is not bondage, but sight. Darkness distorts bad things to seem good and good things to seem bad. As a child, I was very afraid of the dark. I remember climbing into bed with my parents and staring at a corner in their bedroom where there was a dresser against the wall. In the space between the dresser and the wall, I was certain I could see a wolf's eyes peering at me. Sometimes it looked like a tiger. But when the light came on, this was quickly disproved. Likewise, in the dark we are afraid of all kind of things that we shouldn't be. Darkness can have the opposite effect too. You might think you're stroking sweet baby kitties, only to have the lights turned on to discover you've got a rat infestation. Ladies, we need Jesus to see sin as ugly and God as good.

Living in Christ and being united to his perfection and death and resurrection is not burdensome; it is real life and freedom. God gave us a new self in and through Christ, and it is not freedom to try to grasp at the desires of the sin-sick old self. It is not freedom to turn off the light. In 1694 Mary Astell writes in her essay *A Serious Proposal to the Ladies*, "You are therefore Ladies, invited into a place, where you shall suffer no other confinement, but to be kept out of the road of Sin."[39] Is this not the freedom for which Christ paid such a high price? Is this not the freedom he values so supremely? That we "suffer no other confinement, but to be kept out of the road of Sin." And we have this from the apostle Paul:

> For you were called to freedom, brothers. Only do not use your freedom as an opportunity for the flesh, but through love serve one another. (Gal. 5:13)

Once we've tasted the freedom we have in Christ, we learn that we have so much more to learn about what real freedom is. There are heights and peaks to this freedom that we've barely even glimpsed. The desire for this righteous freedom grows and grows the more we taste how sweet it is. As we're set free by Christ to live as Christian women in Christ, to do good works through Christ, we unearth a seemingly infinite joy as we go further up and further in to the infinite Christ. We discover that our lives are never so satisfied and meaningful as they are when we're found hidden in Christ.

Discussion Questions

1. Do you find yourself submitting to (or obsessed with) man-made (or self-made) regulations regarding things such as food, remedies, exercise, or other "things that perish"? Why or why not?

2. How do you think submitting to man-made rules affects you and the people closest to you?

3. What would it look like for you to walk in freedom from man-made rules? In other words, what would it look like for you to be free to be righteous in Christ?

17

The Infinite Christ in Finite Women

Christ in you, the hope of glory. Colossians 1:27

A picture is only that. It's one snapshot of the real life that's happening. All I've been able to give you are snapshots and principles. A wise person once said, "The only constant is change." This is why there is still so much left to unearth that I haven't been able to get to in this book. Because we're changing people amid changing circumstances and changing relationships and changing places, living life in Christ is always taking on new dimensions. Every day we face a new circumstance or a new inkling in ourselves or a new relational dynamic that all must be seen in its proper light: as hidden in Christ, from him, through him, to him, and for him.

It's hard to tell how much our identity is rooted in circumstances—in our job or lack of it, in our kids or lack of them, in our spouse or lack of one—until the circumstances change. Our reactions tell us something about where we stand. Are we here, on earth only? Or are we hidden in Christ, at God's right hand in heaven, more secure and safe than the earth itself?

Yet changes in ourselves and to our circumstances are a gift, not least of all because they reveal our death grip on those parts of who we (no longer) are and our reluctance to walk in the direction God is leading us. They're also a gift because they come from our Father. And our Father isn't in the business of sticking it to his children. He's in the business of loving them, disciplining them, and, yes, changing them through varied means to be more like his Son.

But perhaps the greatest gift God gives us when our circumstances won't stop changing is that he reminds us that we are tucked away in the unchangeable Christ, who is the true constant, outlasting even change (Heb. 13:8). In the change of moving, we can never be taken from his presence. In the change of injury or pain, we cannot escape his sovereign purposes and lovingkindness. In the change of death, we will be raised imperishable in the twinkling of an eye (1 Cor. 15:52). In the unchangeable Christ, every circumstantial change is for our good.

Something, Not All Things

Many of us want someone to tell us exactly what to *do* to be a Christian woman; we want a universal and exhaustive template and checklist, but it doesn't exist. The nature of being Christian women isn't based on what we do but on who we are—who he's made us. The whole world, under the prince of the power of the air, is bent on rejecting how God has made men and women. As Christian women, we need to think long and hard about the direction in which we're leaning. Are we flirting with a subtle version of the outright rebellion of the world, manifested in discontentedness and small obfuscations of the parts of God's Word and design that we want to minimize—the parts that simply refuse to be contextualized to the twenty-first century? Or have we cloaked ourselves in a feminine stereotype that leans into legalism and away from the fullness of God's Word, God's design, and God's mission for us? Sisters, we dare not lean anywhere but deeper into Christ.

Being a Christian woman is *something*—it's a reality that is of great value, much larger than we may have realized—but it isn't *all* things. We are not men and women both. We cannot inhabit both realities, and it is a dangerous thing to try because, while we may think that we're simply trying to be more than a mere woman, it's possible that we're actually trying to be God. The solution to being a mere woman isn't to decide to be a human or a man; it's to remember that there are no mere women. There are only women created by God and in his image.

Will we spend our lives pining to be a nonexistent superhuman, unbound by gender, or will we obey the God who loves us? Will we yearn for flat stomachs when God has given our body a baby to grow? Will we ache for the pastor's pulpit when God has asked us to make a home? Will we long to be the head when God has made us the heart? And are we willing to partner with, come alongside of, and be full participants in all that God calls us to? Are we willing to engage our minds and intellects and convictions, offering them with Berean-like discernment?

Are we willing to be agents of the gospel of Jesus Christ? Are we willing to exercise the gifts God has given us, whether teaching, serving, administrating, giving, counseling with wisdom, exhorting, and on and on, to his glory and for his people, holding nothing back? Are we willing to really have some skin in the game? Or will we hide behind the men and hope that no one expects anything of us? Will we believe we were made to learn directly from the mouth of Jesus, receiving his words as food, like Mary, or will we be too distracted with our self-important work, as Martha was? (Luke 10:38–42).

The Greatest of All Graces

If we're Christian women, there are right and wrong answers to those questions. If we refuse to do what God has asked of us, we rob fellow Christian men and women of needed mothers, sisters, grandmothers, and daughters in the family of God. God is not ambiguous about how he feels about man functioning without woman: it is "not good" (Gen. 2:18). Will we agree with God that we are truly part of Christ's body, with an integral role in God's mission to build up the church and save people through his Son (1 Cor. 12:22)?

We aren't going to do these things perfectly—we will mess up; we will fail. But we can learn and grow. We can take baby steps. We can change. And though who we are changes, *who Christ is for us* never does. We have an unchanging God who has given us unchanging principles in his unchanging Book. We are always being shaped by him and conformed to the perfect image of Christ.

If you take nothing else away from this book, remember this: you have been given the greatest of all graces: Christ himself.[40] You, Christian woman, are in Christ. His death is your death, his life is your life, his perfections belong to you. And in uniting you to him, he took your sin, your guilt, and your punishment and killed them by dying for them. When Christ died, he took death down with him, and when he was raised, he gave us the power over death so that we can die daily to sin—a million small deaths over a lifetime that only ever make us more alive in him than we could have imagined.

Not only are we in the infinite Christ; the infinite Christ is in us (Col. 1:27). We carry in us the hope of glory so that eternity is the drumbeat of the new heart we've been given. We carry in us the hope of glory, and all the while, that hope *carries us* through the dark nights and the unique circumstances we find ourselves in. It's a hope that simply cannot be quenched.

May you, dear reader, find your deepest delight in being what he made you and being found in the One who saved you. There is more joy to unearth and more good to unleash and more comfort to take hold of in the Savior who dwells inside you than this finite, fallen world can contain.

May you, no matter your circumstance or condition, unashamedly receive the gift of being a Christian woman.

> Christ, be with me,
> Christ before me,
> Christ behind me,
> Christ in me,
> Christ beneath me,
> Christ above me,
> Christ on my right,
> Christ on my left,
> Christ where I lie,
> Christ where I sit,
> Christ where I arise,
> Christ in the heart of every man who thinks of me,
> Christ in the mouth of every man who speaks of me,
> Christ in every eye that sees me,
> Christ in every ear that hears me.[41]

Discussion Questions

1. Do you tend to lean toward the rejection of God's ways through worldliness and rebellion or toward the rejection of God's ways through man-made religion and legalism?

2. What would it look like for you to be content and grateful for having been made a woman in Christ in whatever life circumstance you find yourself?

3. What is your biggest takeaway from this book? How might God be leading you to apply it to your life or share it with others?

Acknowledgments

If anyone does not stumble in what he says, he is a perfect man, able also to bridle his whole body. *James 3:2*

I frequently stumble in what I say and what heartache such stumbling produces, which is why James says that "the tongue is a fire, a world of unrighteousness" (James 3:6). Only those closest to me know how much stumbling has happened in the course of writing this book. Out of the abundance of the heart the keyboard types, the pen writes, and the mouth speaks (Matt. 12:34). I owe many thanks to those who have kept watch over my words and endeavored to keep me from stumbling.

First, thanks to my mom, Bea Anderson, and my cousin, Kirsten Christianson, who kept watch over my words by giving me actual quiet times in which to write them. Your cheerful care of our kids when I was needing a few uninterrupted hours to plunk things down made all the difference.

To Barb Waldemar and the young women at Bethlehem College who sat through two talks based on the seeds of this book and asked penetrating questions, I am grateful. My thinking was refined and sharpened through you all.

Thank you to the saints who willingly read early versions of this manuscript and provided valuable insights and encouragements:

Sam Crabtree, Pam Larson, Christy Roberts, and Kristin Tabb. The online world is a cool, weird place, and I'm so thankful for friends I've made there, even friends who were willing to spend time helping me with this: Emily Jensen, Abby Hummel, and Michal Crum.

David Mathis was the first person who told me I should and *could* write this book and to get started. Thanks, David. I am also indebted to Lydia Brownback, the official editor of this book, who is as precise as she is wise.

I'm especially thankful for two theologically astute and gracious couples who read "article versions" of the chapters and also the whole manuscript once it was put together and gave timely feedback and support every step of the way: Daniel and Jessica Souza and Andy and Jenni Naselli. You all are fit for the better city to come, and it's an honor to call you my friends.

To the women of Bethlehem Baptist Church's North Campus, thank you for being doers of the Word and for being atypical lovers of Jesus and God's words and design. You all inspire me.

My husband, Tom, should be awarded the medal that goes to spouses who live through a writer's first book and keep their humor and support and goodwill firmly in place. And if that medal doesn't exist, I hope he'll settle for my lifelong admiration and cooking. Tom makes it easy. He is the kind of man who keeps improving the more you know him better. I wish all women had such a man.

Finally, my gratitude overflows for our children, who haven't read this book. They don't need to read it. They're living it—bumps and all. And, Lord willing, I pray that God would make each of their lives a letter from Christ, written not with ink, but with the Spirit of the living God, not on tablets of stone but on tablets of human hearts (1 Cor. 3:3). Do it, Lord. Write the words that never pass away in the lives of us all.

Notes

1. George Herbert, "Coloss. 3:3 Our life is hid with Christ in God," *George Herbert: Complete Poetical Works* (Delphi Classics, 2015), Kindle ed., loc. 2441.
2. I recognize that the term *feminist* means different things to different people, and not all self-described feminists would agree with what I've put forward here, but I think the generalization holds. What I mean by "victim of 'gendered society'" is someone who believes that culture and nature have imposed harmful ideas about gender and sexuality on her from the outside. She generally views biological sex as a separate reality from gender, but both as soft realities that can be changed. The Christian view does not distinguish gender and sex and understands them both as fixed and assigned realities.
3. Larry Cahill, "Equal ≠ The Same: Sex Differences in the Human Brain," The Dana Foundation, accessed July 13, 2018, www.dana.org/Cerebrum /2014/Equal_%E2%89%A0_The_Same__Sex_Differences_in_the _Human_Brain/.
4. Gnosticism is a second-century heresy that sees the material world and flesh as evil, and that special knowledge given directly from God, and shifted away from the gospel, to be the key to enlightenment and salvation.
5. *Genderqueer* means that men or women do not identify as exclusively female or male and ranges from having multiple gender identities to having no gender identity.
6. *Ontological* means "pertaining to the nature of existence." In other words, our femaleness is more than a role; it incorporates our whole selves.
7. C. S. Lewis, *The Last Battle* (New York: HarperCollins, 1984), 207.

Notes

8. John Bunyan, *The Pilgrims Progress* (Chicago, IL: Moody, 2007), 62.

9. C. S. Lewis, *Mere Christianity* (London: William Collins, 2017), 227.

10. Elisabeth Elliot, *Let Me Be a Woman: Notes to my Daughter on the Meaning of Womanhood* (Wheaton, IL: Tyndale House, 1976), 93.

11. This is an applicable article. Jen Wilkin, "Are Compatibility and Complementarity at Odds?" Jenwilkin.net, accessed July 13, 2018, www.jenwilkin .net/blog/2016/03/are-compatibility-and-complementarity.html?rq= complementarity.

12. "Let a woman learn quietly with all submissiveness. I do not permit a woman to teach or to exercise authority over a man; rather, she is to remain quiet. For Adam was formed first, then Eve; and Adam was not deceived, but the woman was deceived and became a transgressor. Yet she will be saved through childbearing—if they continue in faith and love and holiness, with self-control" (1 Tim. 2:11–15).

13. C. S. Lewis, *The Voyage of the Dawn Treader* (New York: HarperCollins, 1984), 209.

14. Charlotte Brontë, *Jane Eyre* (Mineola, NY: Dover, 2002), 167.

15. Nancy Wilson outlines this train of thought in her address "Dangerous Women," *Femina* weblog, accessed July 13, 2018, www.feminagirls.com /2010/05/29/dangerous-women/.

16. Elisabeth Elliot, *Let Me Be A Woman: Notes to my Daughter on the Meaning of Womanhood* (Wheaton, IL: Tyndale House Publishers, 1976), 34.

17. A helpful article to understanding oppression in marriage is Darby Strickland, "Identifying Oppression in Marriages," *Journal of Biblical Counseling* 30.2 (2016): 7–21, https://www.ccef.org/wp-content/uploads /2016/01/2-IdentifyingOpression-Strickland-Preview.pdf.

18. "Get the Fact and Figures," *The National Domestic Violence Hotline,* accessed July 13, 2018, www.thehotline.org/resources/statistics/.

19. If the law has been broken or you or your children are in danger, and your church doesn't have resources to help you get a safety plan in place, call the National Domestic Violence Hotline at 1-800-799-7233 or TTY 1-800-787-3224, or call the police.

20. G. K. Chesterton, *What's Wrong with the World* (San Francisco, CA: Ignatius Press, 1994), 56.

21. Ibid.

22. J. R. R. Tolkien, *The Fellowship of the Ring* (Boston, MA: Houghton Mifflin, 2002), 32.

23. Elvina M. Hall, "Jesus Paid It All" (1865), Cyberhymnal.org., http://cyber hymnal.org/htm/j/p/jpaidall.htm.

24. David Mathis, "The Cost of Disciple-Making," Desiring God, accessed July 13, 2018, www.desiringgod.org/messages/the-cost-of-disciple -making.

25. Ibid.

26. Dietrich Bonhoeffer, *The Cost of Discipleship* (New York: Macmillan, 1979), 108.

27. Elisabeth Elliot, "The Essence of Femininity: A Personal Perspective," Revive Our Hearts, accessed July 13, 2018, https://www.reviveourhearts .com/articles/essence-femininity-personal-perspective/.

28. Joe Rigney, "Envy and Rivalry in Ministry: The Great Danger Facing the Young, Restless, and Reformed," Desiring God, accessed July 13, 2018, http://www.desiringgod.org/articles/envy-and-rivalry-in-ministry.

29. C. S. Lewis, *Voyage of the Dawn Treader* (New York: HarperCollins, 1984), 183.

30. Joseph Hart, "Come, Ye Sinners, Poor and Needy" (1759), Hymnary.org, https://hymnary.org/text/come_ye_sinners_poor_and_needy_weak _and.

31. Vaneetha Risner, "What Does It Really Mean to be #Blessed?" Desiring God, accessed July 13, 2018, http://www.desiringgod.org/articles /what-does-it-really-mean-to-be-blessed.

32. Ibid.

33. Martin Luther, "Preface to the Wittenberg Edition of Luther's German Writings," Wisconsin Lutheran Seminary website, accessed July 13, 2018, https://www.wls.wels.net/rmdevser_wls/wp-content/uploads /2011/05/Helpful-Articles-Luthers-Preface-to-the-Wittenberg-Edition -of-His-German-Writings-Luther.pdf.

34. J. R. R. Tolkien, *The Fellowship of the Ring* (Boston: Houghton Mifflin, 2002), 379.

35. Marshall Segal, "A Song for the Suffering (with John Piper)," Desiring God website, accessed July 13, 2018, http://www.desiringgod.org /articles/a-song-for-the-suffering-with-john-piper.

36. These cookies are worth the bit of extra effort they require to grind the oats and chocolate bars. You won't regret making them. Find them at Geniuskitchen.com, http://www.food.com/recipe /authentic-mrs-fields-chocolate-chip-cookies-83777.

37. I've given this recipe to more people than I can remember. If you want to make bread but are afraid to try, this is the place to go: Simply So Good, http://www.simplysogood.com/2010/03/crusty-bread.html.

38. C. S. Lewis, *The Weight of Glory* (New York: HarperCollins, 2000), 140.

39. Mary Astell, *A Serious Proposal to the Ladies: For the Advancement of their True and Greatest Interest* (London: King's Head, 1694), Gutenberg.org,

accessed July 13, 2018, http://www.gutenberg.org/files/54984/54984-h /54984-h.htm.

40. I have a recollection that this was something John Owen said, but I can't find the source anywhere.

41. Excerpt from Saint Patrick's Breastplate, Wikipedia.org, https://en. wikipedia.org/wiki/Saint_Patrick%27s_Breastplate.

General Index

Adam and Eve, 48
affliction. *See* suffering
ambassadors, for Christ, 93
ambition, selfish, 99
anti-woman narrative, 38
authority: of Christ, 83, 137; of God, 81; nature of, 83; under, 81

becoming, 31
Bible, the: author of, 44; godly women in, 61; as master, 44; parts of, 45–46; studying, 128; as a whole, 44–45; "women" sections of, 46
blessing(s): of God himself, 128; of suffering, 127
bodies, 49–50; broken, 55; as home, 53; importance of, 56; as living sacrifice, 55–56; natural, 50; as type of revelation, 55; view of, 56

calling, of women, 39
change, in circumstances, 143–44; in ourselves, 144; as gift, 144
child bearing, 56
childlessness, 77
children, gift of, 77–78, 94; spiritual, 107
Christ: being found in, 28; death of, 31; revelation of, 28
church, counsel from, 101

circumstances, appointed by God, 62; change in, 143
comparison, 116
competition, 114
contentment, 121
control, feeling of, 136
creation, 34; of woman, 35–36
critical gender studies, 44
curse, the, 87

darkness, distortion of, 140
death: in Christ, 48–49; to self, 100
dependence, 120; discovering, 128; prayerful, 121; through suffering, 128
desperation, 120, 122
discipleship, 106; irrepressible, 106
discipling, goal of, 107–8; work of, 109
disorder, of mind and heart, 102

envy, 114
equality, not owed, 115
experience, expertise from, 138

faith, measuring, 115–16
faithfulness, 99; learning about, 75
families, and singles, 74
feelings, misfit, 61
feminine, virtues, 41–42
femininity, perception of, 35; manufactured, 40–42

155

Scripture Index